IN FOCUS

GW01006161

PERU

A Guide to the People, Politics and Culture

Jane Holligan de Díaz-Límaco

LATIN AMERICA BUREAU

INTERLINK BOOKS
NEW YORK

This edition first published 2000

In the U.S.:

Interlink Books
An imprint of Interlink Publishing Group, Inc.
99 Seventh Avenue, Brooklyn, New York 11215 and
46 Crosby Street, Northampton, Massachusetts 01060
www.interlinkbooks.com

Library of Congress Cataloging-in-Publication Data

Holligan de Díaz-Límaco, Jane
      Peru in focus: a guide to the people, politics and culture / by Jane
      Holligan de Díaz-Límaco
        p. cm. (The in focus guides)
      Includes bibliographical references and index.
      ISBN 1-56656-232-5 (pbk.)
      1. Peru - Guidebooks. 2. Peru - Description and travel.
      I. Title. II. Series: In focus (New York, N.Y.)
      1998   CIP

In the U.K.:

Latin America Bureau (Research and Action) Ltd,
1 Amwell Street, London EC1R 1UL

The Latin America Bureau is an independent research and publishing
organization. It works to broaden public understanding of issues of
human rights and social and economic justice in Latin America and the
Caribbean.

A CIP catalogue record for this book is available from the British Library

ISBN: 1 899365 17 6

Editing: James Ferguson
Cover photograph: Festival of Corpus Christi, Tony Morrison/South
    American Pictures
Cover design: Andy Dark
Design: Liz Morrell
Cartography and diagrams: Catherine Pyke

Already published in the *In Focus* series:
Argentina, Bolivia, Brazil, Chile, Colombia, Costa Rica, Cuba, Domini-
can Republic, Eastern Caribbean, Ecuador, Guatemala, Jamaica, Mexico,
Nicaragua, Peru, Venezuela

Printed and bound in Korea

CONTENTS

Introduction: The Land of Marvels   **4**

1 ———— **The Country: Worlds Apart**   **7**
City of Kings   *10*
The Coast   *13*
The Sierra   *14*
The Selva   *16*

2 ———— **History: The Ghost of Túpac Amaru**   **18**
The Incas   *20*
A World Turned Upside Down   *23*
Enter the Radical Military   *28*
Fujimori   *31*
Years of Fear   *32*

3 ———— **Economy: Gift of the Devil**   **42**
Exports and Imports   *44*
Coca   *49*
Employment and the Informal Sector   *53*
Economic Power   *53*

4 ———— **Society and People: All the Bloods**   **55**
Discrimination   *55*
Indians of the Selva   *62*
Health   *70*
Crime   *72*
Church   *72*

5 ———— **Culture: Art and Identity**   **75**
Music and Dance   *75*
Media and Politics   *76*
Literature   *78*

Where to Go, What to See   **82**
Tips for Travelers   **87**
Addresses and Contacts   **89**
Further Reading and Bookstores   **90**
Facts and Figures   **91**

INTRODUCTION: THE LAND OF MARVELS

Partygoers getting ready for an elegant reception at the Japanese ambassador's residence in Lima towards the end of 1996 might well have reflected that things were looking up for Peru. Countries like Japan, scared away by terrorist attacks during more than fifteen years of political violence, were now returning as aid donors and investors. Concrete apartment and office blocks shooting skywards in up-market districts of the capital were signs of new hope. It seemed, finally, that uncontrollable inflation and political turmoil were a fading memory.

It took a small band of well-armed and determined rebels just a few minutes to blast their way into the marquee at the residence where the ambassador and a select group of guests were enjoying cocktails. Suddenly, amid the laden buffet tables, armed teenagers masked with the red-and-white bandannas of a tiny, almost-forgotten Marxist group were pinning scores of company directors and diplomats to the ground with sub-machine guns.

Once again, the unthinkable had happened.

Since the sixteenth century, when it was the El Dorado of Spanish fortune-hunters, blinded with greed by its unimaginable gold treasures, Peru has been synonymous with wonder. But, like the wonderland beyond Alice's mirror, it is a world of unpredictable extremes that can be either monstrous or marvelous. Peruvians sum this up in a popular saying: *"Este es el país de las maravillas"* ("this is the land of marvels") or, a looser translation, "anything can happen."

Natural marvels seem endless in Peru, with snow-topped Andean peaks, flocks of dazzlingly blue parrots whirling towards a canopy of rainforest leaves, or dolphins arching offshore during a lull in the crashing waves. Or hundreds of Andean villagers thundering down a hillside with outstretched arms to herd gazelle-like vicuñas into a massive pen, where they will shear them of their fine, soft hair. News of the discovery of Machu Picchu and the unearthing of the tombs of the Lords of Sipán in the desert north, shrouded among delicate gold jewelry and hundreds of watchful pottery offerings, brought fresh reminders in the twentieth century that modern Peru rests on layers of ancient cultures.

In the last three decades, Peru's fame has many times turned to notoriety because of disasters, violence, and drugs. Its varied and extreme geography can turn treacherous. In 1970, an earthquake triggered an avalanche that buried the town of Yungay. This, one of the worst disasters caused by an

Machu Picchu   *Annie Bungeroth*

earth tremor to hit the western hemisphere, killed around 70,000 people as they celebrated a local festival. Peru also hit the headlines when it fostered a radical military dictatorship in the 1960s, led by a left-wing general who wanted to divide the land among the peasants. In later decades it became the world's leading producer of coca leaf, the raw material of cocaine. The emergence of the Maoist-inspired Shining Path rebels, the most brutal of guerrilla groups to take up arms in the region, rent the country apart. The death toll by the mid-1990s was more than 30,000, many of them peasants caught in the crossfire, in the war between the rebels and vengeful military forces. The flux continued with the migration of hundreds of thousands fleeing the violence and with the electoral tsunami which in a few short weeks plucked Alberto Fujimori, the son of Japanese immigrants, from obscurity as an agricultural university rector and carried him to the presidency in 1990. This former dark horse is now setting his sights on one of the longest presidential terms of any Peruvian leader.

Peru's roller-coaster economic history is marked by spurts of export-led wealth and slides into bankruptcy. Meanwhile, spectacular government mismanagement has seen many grandiose plans founder. The concrete stumps of a never-completed elevated railway still limp across Lima, while sections of the jungle highway that President Fernando Belaúnde dreamed would link Peru with Brazil, trail off, unfinished. Economists' charts record how the booms, fired by an abundance of copper, fish, cotton, or fuel, pull up sharply, then tumble away.

Despite this turbulent change and uncertainty, Peru retains its sense of timelessness, keeping intact many of its cultural traditions in its ancient religious beliefs, folk-healers, fiestas, music, dance, and varied cuisine.

Much of life in the Andes and the Amazon has continued regardless. Climbing around the ruins of Pisac in Cusco, tourists might glance down and see peasant farmers tilling and planting by hand the old terraces, which were cut into the mountainside by the Incas. Despite land reform, rebel massacres, and grinding poverty, many people continue to live much as they have done for centuries, isolated in part by their Quechua language, the inhospitable terrain, and, recently, by emergency rule.

Yet the unpredictability of living in Peru is not purely a trick of fate or geography. In his ironic comic strip, *El País de las Maravillas*, cartoonist Alfredo Markos hints that many of the "marvels" of Peru, are caused by corruption and prejudice. His star is a *calato*, a naked man who has been stripped of everything. He lives in a shack with nothing but a television. Like nearly half of Peru's population, he is poor. He can only gape amid a growing crowd on the sidewalk as shop-windows display fancier and fancier goods.

Although the *calato* often crosses paths with the president or his ministers, usually when he is begging or seeking work, in reality Peru is designed so that its different worlds seldom meet. When they do, as when a group of armed teenagers from poor jungle villages, drilled by a former factory worker, became uninvited guests at a Lima embassy party, it is a shocking reminder of the many worlds — the terrifying, ancient, marvelous and mysterious — which still often uncomfortably coexist in Peru.

1   THE COUNTRY: WORLDS APART

Peru has what could be called an all-or-nothing geography, nature taken to extremes. Three distinct geographical regions run north to south. On the coast there is a thin strip of arid desert which is surprisingly fertile where it is broken by narrow river valleys. The *costa* or coastal region makes up just ten per cent of the territory, but is home to about 60 per cent of Peruvians. A broad backbone of brown hills and huge snow-topped mountains fractures the country in two before slipping in the east through rolling green hills of high jungle that drop into a huge expanse of lush rainforest which covers around sixty per cent of the country. Even now, the clear geographical split is also a cultural and psychological one, with most inhabitants considering the *costa, sierra* (highlands), and *selva* (jungle) to be different worlds in every sense.

Few countries can match Peru's natural variety. You can travel inland from the coast, where rarely more than two inches of rain falls a year, eked out in a misty drizzle, over mountain ranges topped by snow and slopes pounded by seasonal heavy rains, on to the hot, wet, and sticky rainforest.

An amazing mix of altitudes and climates means that in Peru there are 84 of the 104 known bio-systems in the world. Desert sands, glaciers, and verdant rainforest exist side-by-side. Peru has jaguars, alligators, sea lions, and vicuñas. It has around a tenth of all the known mammals on the planet and more than a fifth of known birds. In the jungle there is the oddly-beaked blazing red Cock of the Rock, parrots in green and scarlet, yellow and blue. Elsewhere, pink-winged flamingos, majestic, circling condors, waddling Humboldt penguins, and flocks of seagulls are just some of the rich bird life. Peru has an estimated 50,000 plant species, including the world's greatest variety of orchids, and an innumerable array of insects. In only three square miles of Manu National Park in the southeastern rainforest, biologists and botanists have recorded 91 species of mammals, 1,100 different butterflies, 600 types of beetle, and 545 species of birds.

Blessings and Curses

Every October in Lima, thousands of people wearing purple tunics crowd the downtown streets to catch a glimpse of the city's most revered image, a painting of El Señor de los Milagros, the Lord of Miracles. Veiled black women carrying silver chalices of smoking incense accompany the icon, which is paraded through the streets on the shoulders of purple-robed men. Some people follow in wheelchairs, others walk backwards or crawl on their knees. Members of the brotherhood of devotees hold crying babies up close to the image. Street sellers carrying purple coat-hangers strung with luminous rosaries and holy necklaces work their way through the crush. Lining the sidewalks are stalls selling *turrón,* layers of biscuit and sweet *manjar blanco,* covered with sprinkles.

The cult of El Señor de los Milagros grew out of a deep-seated fear of Peru's natural wrath and unpredictability. In October 1746, this religious image painted by a black slave on a wall in 1651 remained standing after an earthquake devastated the capital, leveling most of the buildings. The mural had already survived an earthquake in 1655, and miracles were attributed to it from 1670. October is still considered the month of earthquakes, *temblores* as they are known in Peru.

In a country where earthquakes, flash floods, and landslides come every year, it is not hard to understand Peruvians' deep and ancient respect for the gods of thunder and lightning, the mountains, the land, and the spirits who control the earth. Peru sits on a seismic fault. While the Nazca plate buried deep off the coast of Peru shifts as it sinks underneath the continent, it unleashes powerful tremors. This constant activity means that in 1996, Peru suffered 1,652 seismic movements, of which 66 were strong enough to be felt by its inhabitants. The most devastating of that year happened in

The earthquake at Arequipa, 1868   *London Illustrated News*

April 1996, when a tremor virtually flattened the city of Nazca and several mountain villages inland. A dozen people died. The impact of the natural disaster was greater than it might have been because of the inadequacy of the adobe constructions. Earthquake experts said that the older adobe buildings, constructed with thick walls, survived, while the newer ones, where adobe bricks are modeled on the size of modern fired bricks, were too flimsy to stand up to the quake. The root cause of the destruction was that the smaller bricks are cheaper.

Strange Waters

The waters off Peru are special, but the country's unusually good fortune is offset by a curse. Unlike other countries on the same latitude, Peru's waters are strangely cold. The Humboldt current that flows up the coast of western South America from Antarctica keeps water temperatures low. Cold water from near the sea bed wells up to the surface, chilling the sea. This plankton-rich cold current hosts a huge fish population which in turn supports a whirling variety of birds, including pelicans and seagulls.

The curse is El Niño, a current named after the Christ-child, which sweeps down every few years, warming the waters and driving the shoals away. Changes in ocean temperatures brought on by this current turn rivers into torrents of destruction. The advent of El Niño is for fishermen the equivalent of a drought for farmers. It also affects agriculture because it can drive away rain in the south and cause torrential rains in the north.

Land of Plenty?

There are very few crops that cannot be grown in Peru. A walk round any street market will show the exuberance of fruits and vegetables that Peruvians take for granted. There are dozens of different kinds of potatoes, from the meltingly smooth yellow potato to the pink-tinged *papa huayro*. Peru is home to the potato and Peruvians are potato connoisseurs. Among the familiar apples and oranges are many exotic fruits, from football-sized papayas, knobbly *chirimoyas*, and orange-fleshed *lúcumas* to red or yellow mangoes. From the *ceja de selva* — the high jungle where the sierra meets the selva — there is aromatic coffee and cocoa.

Yet this show of plenty does not mean that the land is without its problems. Although Peru is one of the twenty largest countries in the world, only about fifteen per cent of its land is considered suitable for agriculture or pasture. The lush rainforest conceals one of the most sterile and fragile soils in the world, which has already frustrated development projects, while in the sierra the altitude makes farming on the higher slopes a constant battle. Mountain farmers have to contend with frost, droughts, steep inclines, and increasingly exhausted soil.

There are as many historic reasons as practical ones for this potential farming nation's reliance on food imports, including a general reluctance to eat some traditional sierra produce like the high-protein grain quinoa, a staple associated with the native Andeans. There is no sign that Peru is getting any closer to greater self-sufficiency. Although population growth has slowed from a peak of some 2.4 per cent a year, to 1.7 per cent in 1996, there are still 400,000 new Peruvians each year. Population growth is far higher in poorer, rural areas than in cities. In 1996, imports of wheat, corn, rice, and sugar cost more than $637 million, even though Peru has traditionally been a sugar and rice producing country.

The last four decades have seen Peru shift from being a predominantly rural country to an urban one. More than 70 per cent of Peruvians lived in cities in 1996, compared with 35 per cent in 1940 and 47 per cent in 1961. The scale of the migration, speeded in the 1980s by the eruption of political violence in rural areas, means that cities have grown in anarchic fashion, particularly the capital.

The City of Kings

Love it or hate it, Lima is by far the most important city in Peru. It is now home to nearly a third of all Peruvians and has stretched out into the desert hills on all sides. Far from the tiny city of 69 people founded in 1535 by Francisco Pizarro, who named it the city of kings because it was founded on the Epiphany, sprawling Lima now inspires antipathy among many visitors. British author Nicholas Shakespeare wrote on re-arriving there, "I had forgotten what a vile city Lima was"; the Peruvian playwright and poet Sebastián Salazar Bondy wrote a famous essay, evocatively titled *Lima, la horrible.*

Lima is a city which has burst its banks, which is out of control, a city where the anarchy born of poverty is on every sidewalk. The sand dunes around the city, now crammed with flimsy houses, are more gray than yellow. Lima struggles with a long winter when citizens complain that the fine fog which hangs over the city means they see neither sun nor blue skies for nearly eight months of the year.

Lima's growth is staggering. From a smart, self-confident city with a population of 1.8 million in 1952, Greater Lima has swollen into a vast metropolis of seven million people, around the same population as a country like Switzerland. Including the neighboring port city of Callao, there are probably more than eight million people living in and around the capital. The main split in Peru is not between urban and rural dwellers, but between those who live in Lima and those who do not.

Along with its growth comes the greatest single change in the last decades – a phenomenon that historians are calling the "Peruvianization" or

Central Lima   *Annie Bungeroth*

"Andeanization" of Lima. Andean people have arrived in their hundreds of thousands, fleeing political violence or simply seeking a better living, making the capital reflect the racial mix of the whole country for the first time.

Lima is more than ten times larger than the next biggest city in Peru, Arequipa, and its unchecked expansion has brought a litany of shortages. Water is one of the biggest problems for a capital built in a river valley but surrounded by desert. The Rímac river which attracted the original settlers has only a low water level and is contaminated by the garbage of shanty towns on both sides of its banks. When the rainy season in the mountains is short or when there is a mountain drought, most of Lima suffers water rationing because there is simply not enough to go around. In the younger shanty towns or *pueblos jóvenes* people often wait days for water cistern trucks to arrive selling water. Thirty per cent of its inhabitants have no running water, 60 per cent of properties are not legally registered, and only a quarter of the garbage produced is properly disposed of.

The capital is short of at least 1.8 million houses and most people have taken the solution into their own hands. The most common move for the desperate and homeless is that of *invasiones*, where groups of people organize a takeover of unoccupied desert land, where they form their squatter township. They slip in often under cover of darkness with poles and straw matting, ready to mark out their new home in the sand. The police are often sent in to expel these invaders, more often than not violently. The women and children lead the defense with whistles to warn of approaching police. If successful, the new squatter township becomes an

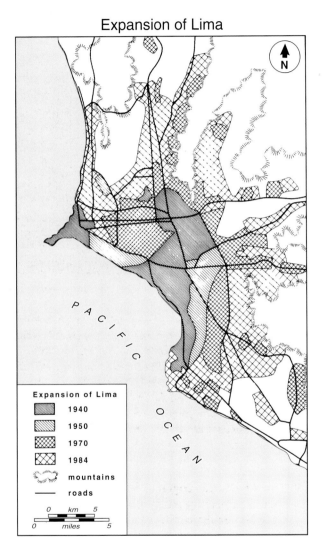

Expansion of Lima

Expansion of Lima
- 1940
- 1950
- 1970
- 1984
- mountains
- roads

0 km 5

0 miles 5

PACIFIC

OCEAN

N

asentamiento humano (settlement). New residents give it a name like Keiko Sofia, after the daughter of President Fujimori, hopeful that its lofty patron might protect it.

The outskirts of Lima have not only been invaded by the poor. Rich suburbs have grown up eastwards, heading towards the Andean foothills. While apartment blocks are replacing houses in Miraflores and San Isidro, houses with swimming pools and large gardens are laid out in residential groups on the road to the Cieneguilla valley east of the city. In these smarter new districts, the names of the new roads could well mirror their residents' social pretensions. Some roads have incongruous names like "Inca Golf Course Avenue." In some areas like La Molina, poor squatter towns and rich *residencias* eye one another from different sand dunes, across the deep economic divide.

Lima's problems are so pressing that it is easy to miss its charm and its historical significance, which goes back beyond Pizarro. Between the smart districts of Miraflores and San Isidro drivers have to take a diversion around a *huaca* or ancient pyramid that still squats among the suburban houses and ice-cream parlors. There are many *huacas* dotted in and around Lima, of which the largest is Pachacamac, a pre-Inca and Inca shrine in the Lurin valley south of the capital.

Reed fishing boats, northern coast

Julio Etchart/Reportage

Even after decades of neglect, there is a faded grandeur to the colonial balconies and pastel-colored houses of the downtown and old districts like Barrios Altos. UNESCO has acknowledged the historic importance of Lima's old center by declaring it a "Cultural Heritage of Humanity." The restoration of the Plaza de Armas and the nearby Plaza de San Martín, along with the relocation of many street traders, has started the long haul to restore the older quarters and draw people back to the area. Although there is much still to be done, people are warming to the idea of "recovering" the long-derided city center.

The Coast

The coast is the smallest of the three geographic regions, but it accounts for the lion's share of economic activity. Apart from mining, most of Peru's export booms have started on the coast, with guano (bird droppings used as fertilizer) and sugar and cotton, which were farmed in the great haciendas or estates that grew up in the coastal strip. Since the early twentieth century, oil production has dominated the economy of the far north of Peru, in Piura and Talara.

A little further south, in the Trujillo and Chiclayo area, the fishermen use *caballitos de totora*, single-person reed boats with sharply pointed tips woven out of the strong totora reed which date back to before the Spanish conquest. Straddling these, fishermen on Huanchaco and Pimentel beach paddle out to sea, using the surf and swell to move away from the beach. The area's agricultural sector is in upheaval after the government forced the 30-year-old sugar cooperatives to become more conventional private limited companies. Newer crops like asparagus and broccoli are proving successful export earners among the agro-industrial estates. Further down the coast, the smell that hangs around the city of Chimbote, heart of the country's fishmeal industry, is enough to tell you what its business is. The industry, one of the country's top export earners, is attracting concern about over-fishing and the practice of swilling waste back into the sea.

South of Lima, the sunny Ica valley is Peru's vineyard. Peruvians are more often beer or spirit drinkers, and their wine generally takes second place to the country's own version of brandy, the clear grape-derived *pisco*, the base of the frothy pisco sour cocktail. Tacna, the most southern city of Peru, was in Chilean hands between 1880 and 1929, when its people voted to return to Peru. The city is a center for contraband, the small-scale smuggling of goods from Chile. However, the steady stream of housewives bringing in suitcases of clothes and electrical goods to sell in Lima's markets has thinned since the government passed special duty-free measures in southern ports.

The Sierra

With its thin mountain air, clay red land, endless twisting roads, river gullies, bright yellow broom, flowering cactus plants, and distant snow peaks, the sierra is harsh and beautiful. The people who live there have to contend with rains, droughts, sharp slopes, and remoteness. Rural life remains simple, with clay adobe houses and many of the same crops that were grown in Inca times like corn, potatoes, *ají* (hot pepper), beans, and quinoa. Many small farmers keep *cuyes* (guinea pigs), often together with a few sheep or llamas. Wild vicuña, a gazelle-like wild cousin of the domesticated llama, and alpaca, with finer hair, have been declared the property of Andean villagers who are learning to herd the flocks once a year and shear their fleece.

Like the sharp natural differences of the region, with its bright sun and deep shadows, the Andean people wear clothes that are full of color and contrasts. The women wear bright *mantas* in which they carry their babies or loads on their backs, while the men have ponchos for the icy nights, usually woven in natural browns or reds, although in some areas brighter colors are used.

With its deep red soil and green pastures, the northern department of Cajamarca is known for its dairy farming and, more recently, for its gold mines. It is also one of the many sites of hot mineral-rich springs famous for their medicinal properties. The most magical contrasts are provided by the

A fertile valley in the Andean region   *Julio Etchart/Reportage*

Ancash department, with its snow peaks and glaciers, turquoise lakes and tropical flowers. As the sierra marches south it widens and conditions become more adverse in the central sierra that was once known pejoratively as the *mancha india* (Indian stain) of Ayacucho, Huancavelica, and Apurimac. The terrain on the higher slopes, known as the *puna*, is a grassland that resists easy cultivation. Indian villagers, growing potatoes, *oca*, and other highland crops, eke out a modest living with a handful of animals.

The central sierra has also been marked by the mining industry which settled there in Cerro de Pasco. Populous mining towns with their own schools, hospitals, and soccer fields have grown up around the largest prospects, even at altitudes of between 9,000 and 12,000 feet above sea level. Around two-thirds of those who live in the central sierra depend on the Cerro de Pasco mining complex for a livelihood.

Nearer to Lima, in the fertile Mantaro valley, lies the prosperous market gardening and trading city of Huancayo. Beyond the valley are the flower fields of the town of Tarma. Cusco, further south, once the heart of a huge Inca empire, still bears the stamp of this culture. Local farmers continue to cultivate some of the terraces cut into the mountains thousands of years ago, although the ancient irrigation systems usually no longer work because of neglect or decay.

Arequipa, in the shadow of the Misti volcano, is physically in the sierra, at more than 7,000 feet above sea level, but psychologically it belongs to the coast. This elegant city is known as the white city because many of its buildings are built of white volcanic rock, called *sillar*. Arequipa has thriving textile and dairy industries. *Arequipeños* are known for their disdain for the rest of the country, and the feeling is mutual. Northeast of Arequipa, lies the Colca Canyon, reputedly the deepest canyon in the world, with its spectacular terracing and Andean villages. Travelers can enjoy views of volcanoes and wheeling condors.

On the southern border with Bolivia, the unremarkable city of Puno stands in contrast to the beauty of Lake Titicaca, the immense, deeply blue stretch of water which is the world's highest navigable lake. This south-

Sawmill factory in the rainforest

Tony Morrison/South American Pictures

ern department marks a change of character, for most of the natives are Aymaras, with a different language and customs from those of the Quechuas to the north. On the lake, half of which belongs to Bolivia, strange man-made islands of totora reed anchored to growing plants are home to the Uros. Deeper into the lake is the island of Taquile, which preserves many indigenous customs, including the men's skills as knitters of alpaca wool. Titicaca, the legendary origin of the first Inca rulers, is also a poignant symbol of the lack of care being taken with natural resources. Sewage being poured into Puno bay is changing the ecosystem and spurring the growth of an algae which is strangling the growth of the totora reed.

The Selva

Although it is in the east, the selva that covers half of Peru is more like its Wild West, its last, most mysterious, frontier. It was the refuge of the last Incas who melted into the rainforest in flight from the Spanish invaders. Legends that they took golden treasures with them which have never been found have added to the mystery surrounding the impenetrable rainforest. The selva is enormous, double the size of the rest of Peru, stretching over an area twice the size of California.

It is easy to forget how accessible the *ceja de selva* (the jungle's brow) is from the sierra region. You slip from the chilly heights of La Oroya, a bleak mining town, into the high jungle in a couple of hours. There have always been contacts between the sierra people and those living in the selva. Coca grown in the high jungle was a sacred Inca plant, while ruling Incas were fond of using things like bright feathers from the jungle. Many sierra farmers also tend crops in the *ceja de selva*, since the crops have different harvest times.

Large parts of the area are still unknown to Peruvians, except perhaps to a few of the indigenous tribes which are believed to be uncontacted. Among these are the Nahuas in Madre de Dios, the Ahuatiya in Ucayali, and the Cacatayo in Kashibo, who shun the encroaching woodcutters, biologists, oil explorers, and missionaries. Most of the jungle is inaccessible by land, and life revolves around the rivers which snake through the forest, including the Amazon, the world's longest river, which begins its journey to the sea in Peru. Iquitos, the principal city of the jungle, can only be reached by river or by air.

Much of the variety of Peru's natural life is in the jungle, where vast national reserves like Manú and Tambopata are home to thousands of animal, bird, and plant species which have disappeared from outlying areas. There are also around 300,000 native people living in the jungle, who belong to 65 distinct ethnic groups. Of these the largest are the Aguarunas, with around 45,000 people, and the Ashaninka with around 40,000.

In true Wild West-style, the selva has a reputation for lawlessness. Only around ten per cent of Peruvians live there, including a cast of drug traffickers, wildcat gold prospectors, colonists seeking a better future, and native jungle Indian tribes, still trying to preserve a hunting-and-fishing lifestyle that is increasingly under pressure from outside. Conservationists are also concerned that oil exploration has been given priority over preserving the jungle's ecosystem.

The Borders

Despite their differences, Peruvians take a united view when it comes to their country's borders. Peru is bordered by Ecuador and Colombia to the north, Brazil and Bolivia to the east, and Chile to the south. Simmering disputes about Peru's northern and southern coastal borders mean that relations with Ecuador and Chile remain mired in distrust, despite trade and political pacts pointing to closer regional links.

In the south, Peruvians still regard Chile as having stolen their nitrate fields in the War of the Pacific, and memories of the 1881-3 Chilean occupation of Lima still rankle. More volatile, however, is the relationship with Ecuador where the dispute focuses on a 50-mile-long unmarked stretch of the northern border. Ecuador has fostered territorial ambitions in Peru for decades, and Peruvians are not slow to respond. Since the Rio de Janeiro Treaty, which Quito disowns, was signed in 1942, resentment has boiled over into two border conflicts in 1981 and 1995. The latter month-long undeclared war left dozens dead on both sides and nine aircraft shot down.

2   HISTORY: THE GHOST OF TUPAC AMARU

Tantalizing glimpses of Peru's early history are scattered across the country. They lie in graves, in fashioned gold and lavish cloth, in grinning pottery jugs, in adobe pyramids and majestic cut-stone temples, and in vast, puzzling shapes etched in the coastal desert, but only clearly discernible from the air. Deciphering these codes is not easy since no pre-Columbian Peruvian culture kept any written records. The closest approximation to written texts were the *quipu* or knotted string records of the Incas, and images woven into cloth by indigenous Andeans which some investigators believe might have formed the basis of a pictorial alphabet. Yet despite a lack of recorded evidence, it is known that, from the earliest hunter-gatherers, there have been people living in the country for at least 10,000 years.

Early Cultures

The Inca civilization, found by the Spaniards when they arrived on the Peruvian coast, has eclipsed the many cultures that went before it because it was preserved in the writings of the European soldiers, priests, and travelers. An aggressive nation, based in the southern Andean city of Cusco, the Incas had spread their empire with unprecedented zeal, reaching as far as Quito in the north and central Chile in the narrow southern tail of the region. Yet their rule, when the first Spanish soldier landed on an exploratory expedition in 1528 in Tumbes, was only a couple of centuries old. They had assimilated many other cultures, like the Chimu and the coastal cult of Pachacamac, wrapping them into a tight web of tribute and mutual responsibility.

Then, as now, regional differences were crucial to understanding the whole of Peru, and the legacy of advanced cultures like that of Chavín, the Moche, the Tiahuanaco, and the Wari has not been fully unraveled. There were 4,000 years of cultural development preceding the Inca empire, the country's most famed civilization. Many of these pre-Inca people developed sophisticated skills, like the textile-weaving prowess of the coastal Paracas culture, the metalwork of the Lambayeque culture, and medical techniques which allowed some cultures apparently to perform delicate surgery.

Their advanced level of development is evident from the structures they built, many of which still survive today. The Cupisnique people of the northern coast built platform-mound temples of stone with adobe paintings of fearsome beings with feline-like jaws. This culture is believed to have been the inspiration behind the intriguing Chavín de Huántar temple built

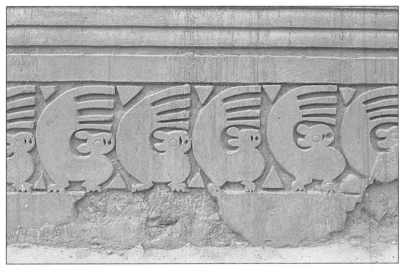

Carvings at Chan Chán   *Chris Hudson*

by the Chavín culture (c.1000-200 BC) high in the Andes in modern-day Ancash, a religious site at a crossroads between the jungle, mountain, and coast. With its underground tunnels and sunken circular courtyard, this temple was probably a center of worship and pilgrimage for a large part of the country. Its feline gods, and exotic images of caymans and cactus plants blended rainforest, coast, and highland images.

The Moche (from around the birth of Christ) in northern Peru are best known for a large collection of ceramics which portrayed their everyday life. Life-like portraits of their people, even including physical defects, are an enchanting record of an artistic people, who languished around 800 AD. They also built the Sun and Moon Pyramids near modern Trujillo, with once-brightly painted walls rising up to 130 feet above the valley floor, which are now being restored. The later Chimu founded their capital, called Chan Chán, in the same valley around 900 AD. During its heyday between 1350 and 1400 AD this series of adobe royal compounds stretched over almost thirteen square miles.

With its long and largely uncharted history, Peru has not lost its allure as a country that is still not completely discovered. Many important and impressive sites have only been found within the last century, recovered from obscurity on cloud-wrapped mountain peaks, like the citadel of Machu Picchu, apparently a late site of worship never discovered by the Spaniards, and the last Inca city of Vilcabamba, uncovered under dense jungle undergrowth. Legends of lost cities have bloomed in Peru since the early sixteenth century and explorers are still convinced that much more remains to be found. Peru's archaeological past, like its natural resources, is in many ways a bounty squandered. The aridity of the desert has preserved many marvels of ceramics, textiles, and gold, but authorities have been powerless to stop the steady pilfering by *huaqueros*, the grave-robbers who loot and sell the treasures, most of which have ended up in private collections, often abroad. Lack of resources has also meant that many ruins stand abandoned.

It is hard to rank some of this century's finds as "discoveries," since in almost all cases local people knew of the buildings' existence. However, indifference, fear of spirits, or lack of understanding of the sites' historical significance kept their existence veiled from archaeologists. Intriguing too, is how elements of ancient Peruvian culture are still evident today in dress, traditional dishes, and customs. The national fish dish, *cebiche*, raw fish marinated in lime juice, also dates back to early coastal cultures, and textile techniques, developed to a fine art by these cultures, are practiced by mountain weavers today. Undoubtedly many ancient spiritual beliefs remain tied in with Andean peasants' deep respect for the natural world, where worship of mountains, the earth, stars, and thunder remains cloaked, but present, in newer traditions.

The Incas

Some would claim that Peru's system of government has headed steadily downhill since the Spanish conquest of the Incas in 1532. The Incas ruled with an authoritarianism balanced by a sense of fairness. The main success of this mountain-based people was their keen organizational skill. Although they had neither writing nor the wheel, the Incas managed to dominate other sophisticated cultures and weave them into their empire with a balance of brutality, threats, tolerance of local religious cults, and offers of stability from the well-run farming and storehouse system.

Faced with a hostile environment, the Incas domesticated the steep slopes and long distances that separated Cusco from its hinterland with vast ter-racing on mountains, irrigation systems, and a network of communica-tions which stretched through the entire empire. The Inca roads were nar-row and punctuated by long suspension bridges and river punts. Strings of chasquis or relay-running messengers could carry messages at dizzying speed across the empire. Contemporary Spanish writers were impressed by the Incas' tax system which, they said, was finely balanced, extracting only what each community could afford to give. The Incas' use of the *mita* or communal workforce also allowed the construction of temples, fortresses, walls, and other buildings in a style still capable of inspiring awe. Huge

stones dragged from distant quarries were locked together so closely that one cannot fit a sharp knife in the join.

While the Incas' statecraft was highly developed, their society was in no way equivalent to the socialist utopia some observers perceive. The speed with which some conquered people switched to supporting the invading Spaniards is a reminder that the Incas were also invaders in other lands.

The Spanish Takeover

How a small band of Spanish adventurers, led by the illegitimate and illiterate soldier of fortune from Extremadura, Francisco Pizarro, became the *conquistadores* of Peru, is a classic tale of duplicity, greed, and determination. First, the Spaniards were lucky to land in 1532, when they returned to Peru with dreams of conquest, at a time when the Inca empire was wracked by a civil war between the brothers Atahualpa in the north and Huascar in Cusco, the Imperial City. Their father, Huayna Capac, had died from a disease, possibly smallpox, which had killed hundreds of his followers.

Pizarro, with 62 horsemen and 160 foot soldiers, was invited by an envoy of the Inca to meet Atahualpa at his army camp near the northern city of Cajamarca, a fertile valley high in the Andes. Afraid but lured by untold riches, the Spaniards rode into the area, where between 40,000 and 80,000 Inca soldiers were camped. The Inca agreed to meet Pizarro the following day. As Atahualpa was carried on a litter into the square, where mounted Spaniards were waiting concealed inside buildings, Spanish priest Vicente de Valverde approached the Inca with a bible and tried to explain that he was the bearer of the Christian faith. Atahualpa was suspicious and although he examined the holy book offered to him, let it fall to the ground. The priest ran back to the Spaniards calling on God, and the Spanish horsemen rode out among the thousands of Incas accompanying the royal litter. Amid carnage of epic proportions, the Spaniards killed the carriers of Atahualpa's litter again and again, but waves of fresh followers took the place of those who fell. The Spaniards met no armed resistance and thousands died or were maimed by Spanish swords or suffocated in the rush to escape. Atahualpa was captured.

Túpac Amaru, the last Inca

An act of deception followed the massacre. Pizarro promised to free the Inca if he filled a room with gold and two with silver. Precious metal in all forms was brought from all over the empire, but to no avail. The Spaniards killed Atahualpa on July 26, 1533, garroting him after he converted to Christianity.

It was the very nature of the Inca empire and the civil war that allowed Pizarro to build on this audacious start and take over Cusco. Disaffected subjects of the empire went over to the Spanish side, swelling the ranks of the conquerors, while on entering Cusco they initially met no resistance because they had toppled Atahualpa, Huascar's rival. The Spaniards ransacked the imperial city to establish their rule. It was the efficiency of the empire that allowed them to take over and run the land smoothly. At first concerned only with golden treasures, the conquistadors found that when they settled they could appropriate the *mita* or labor tribute system to make the collective workforce work for them in the silver mines, discovered later in Potosí.

Inca Resistance

Although Pizarro installed a puppet Inca and found many collaborators among the Inca ruling class, he also encountered resistance. Manco Inca, a son of Huayna Capac, initially became an ally but his relationship with the Spaniards soured. After several heroic battles and a siege in which he nearly recovered Cusco in 1536, he retreated with many of his followers to found an Inca state within the new Spanish-ruled land at Vilcabamba. Manco Inca did not cut off all contact with the Spaniards and permitted two priests into the new Inca state, but retained control of his enclave. After he died, his son Titu Cusi and finally another son, Túpac Amaru, continued to rule there, but this became intolerable for the Spaniards, who decided to ransack the Inca enclave. They finally captured Túpac Amaru in 1572 and he was beheaded in Cusco square, crushing the last defiant Inca kingdom. The public execution, however, failed to fulfill the Spaniards'

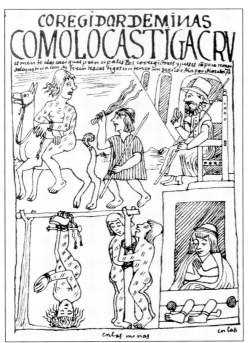

COREGIDORDEMINAS
COMOLOCASTIGACRV

The Spaniards torture Inca mine workers

Courtesy of South American Pictures

hope of extinguishing the spark of resistance. The killing of Túpac Amaru, who converted to Christianity and retained his royal dignity to the last, drew immediate sympathy from most of Cusco and caused great sorrow among native Peruvians. It also ignited a long-smoldering fuse of discontent which meant that there were few rebellions in the Andes that did not later invoke the name of the last Inca.

A World Turned Upside Down

The arrival of the Spaniards turned the Inca empire upside down. In the years following the invasion millions died, mostly from epidemics brought by the Europeans, against which they had no natural immunity. Estimates of the population disaster vary, but most modern historians agree that of a population of between nine and twelve million at the time of the Spanish arrival, only half remained a century later. Others say the drop was even more drastic, with some contemporary estimates calculating that only 1.8 million people were left in Peru by the end of the sixteenth century.

Pizarro shifted the center of the empire from the Andean capital of Cusco to the coast, to the city of Lima, founded on the Rímac river in 1535. He dragged Peru into the world of foreign trade, with exports based at first on looted Inca metals and later on the silver mined in Potosí, in modern Bolivia. The regime imposed by the Spaniards, with heavy taxation and forced labor in mines where conditions were appalling, caused even more deaths. Some of the European clergy who arrived were outraged by the treatment of the natives and protested, but in general, the lot of the Indians improved little.

There were a few who prospered under Spanish colonial rule, but these were isolated cases. Most of the natives lived far removed from Lima or the colonial cities like Cusco and Ayacucho, where courtly life was based on a taste for European things. Finery, bull-fights, and black slaves were common features of life in Lima. The women, known as *las tapadas*, adopted an Arabic-style custom of wearing shawls which covered all their face except for one eye.

Under the determined administration of Viceroy Francisco Toledo, who arrived in 1570, the Inca community was broken up even further, with the people who lived in the countryside forcibly congregated into Spanish-style new towns to make tax collection and conversions to Christianity easier.

Túpac Amaru II

To the people of the Inca empire, their ruler was not a mere king, but a god. This belief, along with the cruel treatment meted out by the conquistadors, explains entrenched resistance to Spanish rule. In the eighteenth century there was more than one uprising based on the messianic promise that the Inca would return, but the most famous was that led by Túpac Amaru II, the name taken by an Inca noble called José Gabriel Condorcanqui.

A portrait of Túpac Amaru shows him in Spanish finery, riding a horse and wearing a plumed hat. Only his dark skin and long black hair give away his Inca ancestry. He identified with his Inca predecessors, claiming to be a direct descendant of Huayna Capac, and led a campaign to protest against Spanish abuses that snowballed into a revolution. Although the uprising found support among other wealthy Indians, peasants, and fugitive black slaves, Túpac Amaru did not win the backing of the *criollos*, the descendants of Spaniards born in Peru. He was eventually caught and retribution was brutal. He was beheaded and quartered in Cusco, the four severed parts of his body displayed in different places that had taken some part in his rebellion. In the aftermath of the uprising the Spaniards also clamped down on many of the lingering Inca traditions, trying to ban the Quechua language, local idols, and Inca dress.

Yet the death of Túpac Amaru gave new strength to the Inkarri myth, remembered by some *campesinos* even today. According to the myth, the Inca's body will be reconstituted and he will return to lead a triumphant revolt. Contrary to an image of complacency, the native Indians of the *sierra* have proved again and again they are willing to rally to the call of insurgency, particularly given the poor conditions in which many peasant communities live.

Somos libres

Peru was swept along in the nineteenth-century South American campaign to break away from Spain. Domestic resentment of the Spaniards had grown among the local *criollos*, who eventually rallied to the call of the *libertadores* — Simón Bolívar in Venezuela and José de San Martín in Argentina. It was an uprising centered on civil servants and merchants who rankled at being passed over by the Spanish elite, recent changes in tax laws, and the removal of Lima's monopoly on trade with Europe.

The declaration of independence made in Lima by Bolívar on July 28, 1821 is still celebrated annually as the anniversary of Peru's liberation from Spanish rule. But the battles continued and only on December 9, 1824, on the plains of the Andean mountain village of Quinua, outside Ayacucho, did the liberators, including many Andean peasants, fight the decisive battle that secured independence for Peru and all of America. The site is marked by a huge white obelisk on the high pampa of Quinua, which can be seen from planes which land at Ayacucho airport. Every December, schoolchildren re-enact the heroic battle at Quinua, a small village of craftsmen which also has a museum of artifacts from the Independence Wars period.

What is perhaps most extraordinary about Peru's independence is how little changed in its wake. The hand-over of leadership was no revolution, and once a disillusioned Bolívar retired to Colombia in 1826, reforms decreed by the liberator, like granting property rights to individual Indians, were rolled back. The *criollo* elite ensured that the Spanish privileges they had so resented remained, but were handed over to them. The economy slumped and veterans of the Independence Wars fought to retain power in a fresh bout of political see-sawing. Between 1826 and 1865, Peru had 34 presidents, including 27 military officers.

From Guano Boom to War

The unlikely savior of the languishing and unstable country was bird dung, known as guano, collected for use as fertilizer in Europe. The boom it spurred allowed the country to get back on its feet, but government overspending meant that when the cycle ended Peru had tumbled back into recession. As the economic crisis hit home, the country tripped into the most catastrophic war of its history, the War of the Pacific. Chilean troops invaded Lima in 1881, and attacked the north as well.

The clearest sign of the complete collapse of Peru's government is that the Chileans could not find a leader with the authority to sign a peace treaty. One intrepid leader, Andrés Cáceres, fled to the central sierra, where landowners at first, and then Indian villagers in droves joined a guerrilla war against the Chileans. Cáceres' *Montoneros* proved the effectiveness of such warfare in the mountainous terrain, but the campaign turned sour when peace was signed with Chile. The deep racial divisions of the country came to the fore when prominent landowners and eventually Cáceres himself turned on the guerrilla army and repressed its troops, unmasking the deep-seated fear in the landowning elite of armed Indians.

A reception for President Leguía, 1925

Aristocracy, Autocracy and Military caudillos

From the ashes of the country left behind by the devastating war with Chile, a new more modern Peru emerged. Copper and cotton became the country's leading export earners. Foreign power groups formed around these industries also grasped political power, ushering in what was perhaps the most stable phase of Peru's turbulent history. Historian Jorge Basadre coined the term the Aristocratic Republic, for the period lasting until 1919 when a succession of civilian presidents linked to the elite, with the exception of one year of military rule, were elected to office.

The smooth pattern crumbled in 1919 when Augusto B. Leguía, a classic populist *caudillo* or strongman politician, won the presidency for a second time. Leguía came to office at a time when the effects of the First World War and the Bolshevik Revolution in Russia were being felt in South America. This tiny man (he was only five feet tall) showered Peruvians with populist measures which earned him such titles as the "Titan of the Pacific." He won the approval of the working class, who benefited from the new eight-hour day and jobs in construction schemes, of the middle class, who entered the growing bureaucracy, and, the Indians, lured by the creation of the *Dia del indio* and the long-overdue legal recognition of their communities. Leguía ran up a huge foreign debt to fund an ambitious infrastructure program and expanded the state's influence and his own political clout. Increasing social and labor unrest, however, led him to abandon much of his reformist program and he brutally repressed opponents.

Leguía also set a trend for political illegitimacy, engineering his stay in power for eleven years and turning democratic rule into a dictatorship. Leguía was ousted in August 1930 by army commander Luís Sánchez Cerro, beginning a new period of alternating military and civilian governments which lasted as late as 1980.

The Mass Parties

As Leguía turned from reform to repression, two of Peru's most influential political thinkers were founding parties whose far-reaching influence on mass politics would stretch through to the end of the twentieth century. The two were Victor Haya de la Torre, founder of the APRA party, and José Carlos Mariátegui, founder of the Peruvian Socialist Party, later to become the Peruvian Communist Party.

The two were very different, but started from the same inspiration: Karl Marx. Mariátegui, a wan-looking, self-taught intellectual, who began working at the age of fifteen at a Lima newspaper, quickly rose to become one of the capital's most incisive journalists. Exiled by Leguía in 1919, he immersed himself in the writings of Marx, Engels, and Lenin during four years in France and Italy. On his return to Peru he published his classic work, *Seven Interpretive Essays on Peruvian Reality* (1928), an attempt to transfer Marxism into a Peruvian context. He incorporated some aspects of the *indigenista* movement, which exalted the qualities of indigenous Andean culture, into his view that capitalism and imperialism were exploiting the country's resources. For Mariátegui, the Andean *campesinos* and the working class would be the backbone of any revolution.

Mariátegui's Peruvian Communist Party (PCP) later spawned many leftist schisms, including the mainstream electoral coalition, United Left (IU), and another group which believed in the revolutionary role of the Andean peasantry: the Peruvian Communist Party for the Shining Path of José Carlos Mariátegui. This was the full official name of the armed group formed in the 1970s which would win notoriety as the Shining Path guerrillas.

Before his early death in 1930, Mariátegui joined forces with Haya, who had moved to university in Lima from the sugar-growing north, but they soon parted ways. Haya preached an amorphous mix of anti-imperialism, nationalism, and Latin American unity which softened and moved rightwards as he aged. In its early years, the party he founded in exile in Mexico, the American Popular Revolutionary Alliance (APRA), spread like an evangelical religion, under his rousing slogan, "Only *Aprismo* will save Peru." Haya talked of sacrifice, historic mission, and union between peasants, workers and the middle class, claiming in one famous speech that, "Aprismo means a new Peru arising." The party was seen by the country's leaders as a serious threat and it was brutally repressed. An insurrection by Apristas in Trujillo in 1932, where 60 army officers were killed, ended with an army clamp-down where hundreds were murdered by night-time death squads in Chan Chán, the ancient adobe fort city, near Trujillo. Noone knows how many were executed. The bitter repression fired the increasingly violent movement's sense of mission and a deep hatred between the army and APRA.

Against the background of greater mass participation in politics, Peru returned to electing a civilian president in 1963. The victor, Fernando Belaúnde Terry of the Popular Action (AP) party, was later depicted by a cartoonist as peering down on ordinary Peruvians from a cloud. The dignified southerner, an architect prone to lofty turns of phrase, failed to realize his grand plans to build a jungle highway reaching Colombia, Venezuela, and Bolivia and to colonize the Amazon. Belaúnde was hindered by a congressional alliance between APRA and the supporters of an old enemy and former dictator, General Manuel Odría. As foreign debt spiraled because of the huge building program, again the unthinkable happened.

Enter the Radical Military

Military coups were no novelty for Peru, but General Juan Velasco's seizure of power in October 1968 shocked not only the country, but the whole region. Suddenly the country had a leader in uniform who saw himself as an ally of the poor. Velasco headed what he called a "revolutionary government" which, at least initially, terrified foreign investors and the local elite.

Velasco's coup marked an abrupt departure from traditional pro-business policies. He immediately took over the oil installations of the U.S.-owned International Petroleum Company, offering no compensation, and followed with expropriations of the mining giant, the Cerro de Pasco Corporation, and the iron mines of the Marcona Mining Company, both U.S.-controlled. Yet the most radical move was announced on June 24, 1969, when the general told a stunned nation that the land must be for those who work it. The great *haciendas* of the agricultural elite were to be broken up and transformed into peasant cooperatives. Velasco ended his televised message, "Peasant, the Master will no longer feed off your poverty."

Velasco raised great expectations among the country's rural and working classes, but his grandiose reforms were not as successful as he had hoped. Although the rural elite was largely dismantled or pushed into other business, production on the land dropped as the smaller farmers continued subsistence farming and the cooperatives' management of agricultural exports was hampered by infighting and lack of know-how. Foreign debt mounted. Shop shelves became increasingly bare as Velasco imposed price controls and import limits. Despite the pomp of ubiquitous military parades, the country became a more dour and dangerous place. Schoolchildren across the country were ordered to wear the *uniforme único*, gray pinafores or pants which are still a feature of state schools. The expropriation of the *Expreso* and *Extra* newspapers was followed by the government seizure of all newspapers, magazines, radio, and television. The media were fed with propaganda by a state machine, which was packed with supporters of the military government.

Lima streets became increasingly unruly as Velasco became more authoritarian. As the country tumbled into yet another economic trough, unrest spread with a police strike and riots in which around 200 people were killed. The military grew discontented too, and a more moderate group of officers staged a bloodless coup in August 1975 against an ailing Velasco. Ultimately the general had lacked planning to follow through his radical reforms, but nevertheless he changed the face of the country by bequeathing to the working and peasant classes a greater sense of their rights and a readiness to protect them.

Back to Democracy

As the new military government swung right, the streets of Lima and other cities seethed with strikers, student protesters, and anarchists in 1977. An attempt to stabilize the economy by embracing the International Monetary Fund and its structural adjustment policies only stoked worse protests in an increasingly radicalized country.

Finally the military held elections for a constituent assembly in 1978, and in 1980 the country returned to civilian rule with the election of Belaúnde for a second term. A more conservative Belaúnde continued his drive to build new projects in the jungle, demanding higher state spending, while he opened up the country's markets and allowed foreign firms to remove profits from the country wholesale. Economic disarray and the debt crisis which was sweeping across Latin America did not spare Peru, where inflation rocketed out of control. Belaúnde turned to the time-honored recipe of IMF austerity, which proved self-defeating as recession hit exports and tax revenues and the economy sank deeper downwards. In 1985 Peru's foreign debt stood at a staggering $14 billion.

APRA's Turn

With his wide smile and outstretched hands, youthful APRA leader Alan García symbolized hope for Peruvians that year, when he was elected president by a landslide. "Alan," as he was familiarly known, was a charismatic speaker and an opportunist fond of grand gestures. A populist par excellence, García was also the youngest-ever Peruvian president and the first head of the APRA party to win office, ending a half-century's wait. Yet García possibly ranks as one of Peru's greatest disappointments. He is still blamed for instilling Peruvians with a deep-seated distrust of politics and politicians.

Turning away from the technocratic Belaúnde's ties with the IMF, in July García dropped a sudden and unexpected bombshell on the foreign banks which had tied up billions in Latin American economies during the 1970s. He announced that Peru would limit its foreign debt payments to ten per cent of its export earnings, raising fears among bankers that he would set a bad example which other indebted nations in the region might follow.

Policies aimed at stimulating domestic consumption fostered a two-year spurt of spectacular economic growth in 1985 and 1986. Yet this boom rapidly ran out of steam, with foreign reserves tumbling and credit lines drying up as Peru became a pariah among the international financial community. After 1987, inflation romped ahead and the value of wages slumped. Large-scale corruption thrived at all levels of the state sector, where the payroll was stuffed with phantom employees paid for political favors. Even big companies negotiated their foreign exchange with the dollar barons of Jirón Ocoña, a side street in central Lima where moneychangers parade with signs saying, "I change torn, ripped, or old dollar bills."

In 1987, García's decision to nationalize the banking industry backfired. Bankers from Lima's traditional elites became popular heroes as they personally barred entry to the military, staring down tank guns and spurring a liberal protest movement led by internationally renowned author, Mario Vargas Llosa. Yet the real moment when the bubble burst was the *paquetazo* or reform package of September 1988. A series of draconian economic measures, including import tariff hikes, devaluation, and foreign exchange controls, was intended to tackle run-away inflation of 500 per cent. The result was that most people's real spending power was cut in half overnight, and Peruvians woke the next day, not knowing the new worth of the money in their pocket. Many spent hours in lines for basic goods and began to hoard items like sacks of sugar or powdered milk. In poorer districts, residents organized *ollas comunes*, communal soup kitchens, to survive.

As reserves were wiped out, inflation continued to reach dizzy figures, with prices soaring by 40 per cent a month. García's populist rhetoric could not deter criticism, particularly as evidence of graft and rumors of multi-million dollar accounts in Swiss banks mounted. Even his image as a man of the masses suffered as he appeared incapable of reining in the dirty war tactics of a military determined to put down insurgency in the Andes. In the mountains, thousands were killed or disappeared in brutal attacks from both sides of the rebel-military war. In Lima, García permitted the massacre of hundreds of rioting Shining Path prisoners when military forces put down prison uprisings in two top-security prisons in July 1986, seriously tarnishing his human rights record.

García ended his term in disrepute and fled into exile in 1992 during political turmoil. He also left many Apristas convinced that the former golden boy had done more to destroy the party than decades of hostile governments which had pursued and outlawed it.

Fujimori

In many ways, the 1990 elections were Peruvians' revenge against traditional politics. In a gesture of almost complete disillusionment, people turned against the leading presidential candidate, world-famous novelist Mario Vargas Llosa, and elected Alberto Fujimori, the rector of Lima's agrarian university, who spent most of his campaign on top of a tractor touring shanty towns. Vargas Llosa failed because he offered an already battered people another shock program of "devaluation" as part of his neo-liberal policies, but his real weakness was that the mass of Peruvians saw him as surrounded by the old rightist parties and the *blanquitos,* the elites of European descent who had held power for years. Tales that Vargas Llosa had enlisted his maid and gardener to act in campaign advertising as shanty town dwellers did not help his popular image. Fujimori, with his clipped and stilted Spanish, the son of Japanese immigrants, won because he was an outsider and struck a chord with Indians, blacks, and other ethnic Peruvians. Embracing his new nickname, *El Chino*, Fujimori promised "work, honesty, and technology" and independence from any of the traditional political parties. His own party, Cambio 90, small and ideologically unclear, was at least untainted by failure and corruption.

Given his status as a complete unknown in 1990, it is remarkable how completely Fujimori has come to dominate the country's politics. He announces new laws while he visits shanty towns to inaugurate schools or climbs to mountain villages to check on irrigation works. It is not rare for him to take both ministers and Congress by complete surprise.

Yet for all his efforts to portray himself as a new style of leader, Fujimori owes much to time-honored political practices. Having arrived in the presidency without powerful party backing or a proper team of policy-makers, Fujimori immediately recognized that the economic chaos he had inherited and the spiraling rebel violence needed drastic solutions. Going back on his electoral promise, he administered the so-called "Fujishock," the same radical package of price rises and currency devaluation which his defeated opponent had proposed. Turning overnight from moderate reformism to ultra-liberalism, Fujimori pledged to slash tariff barriers and privatize all state companies. Frustrated by congressional foot-dragging on most of his measures, he took his greatest gamble and with army support carried out the so-called *autogolpe* or self-coup in April 1992. He dissolved parliament, sacked Supreme Court judges, and took the reins of power, incurring some international protest, but little popular opposition at home. Fujimori's self-coup succeeded largely thanks to the backing of the armed forces' strongman, General Nicolás Hermoza, who remains in charge of the High Command and appears to have moved himself into an unassailable position through his support for the palace coup.

While Fujimori's economic policies resulted in further hardship for Peru's poor, his popularity paradoxically remained high among many of those most adversely affected by the trebling of prices on basic goods and mounting unemployment. Success in taming inflation accounted for some of this popularity, as did the popular perception that Fujimori was attacking the corrupt political establishment by closing down Congress. There is no doubt that his IMF-endorsed policies of a sound, controlled currency, of attracting external investment, of bringing order to the fiscal mess, and reducing the state's role in the economy pulled Peru out of the economic low point where it languished in 1990. Yet the cost for many Peruvians has been extremely high, and poverty remains the country's single biggest problem. But perhaps Fujimori's greatest personal success was a spectacular turnaround in the fight against subversion with the fortuitous capture later in 1992 of Shining Path leader Abimael Guzmán. The arrest of Guzmán, who had acquired almost mythical status, gave Fujimori huge political capital.

Years of Fear

Watched by the massed ranks of the Lima press, a drape over an enormous circus-style cage was lifted to show a bespectacled, bearded middle-aged man, pacing inside. Wearing a striped prison suit like those worn by cartoon convicts, the captive turned towards the press and began to shout a political message. At his words some of the reporters began singing the national anthem. The man was Abimael Guzmán, "Presidente Gonzalo," the most wanted fugitive in Peru, the supreme leader of the Maoist Shining Path rebel group. With his capture in September 1992, twelve years after it began its armed fight to overthrow the Peruvian state, Shining Path had suffered its worst blow, a near-fatal hit.

Nothing this century has changed Peru so much as Shining Path. This Maoist-inspired guerrilla group was responsible for triggering violence which cost around 30,000 deaths and damage to infrastructure estimated at $25 billion since 1980. Shining Path's armed struggle accelerated the

Guzmán caged   *Ana Gonzalez/Reportage*

flight from the countryside to the cities and the disintegration of other, rival left-wing parties. As mayors were killed and others resigned in droves, the military established direct control over huge tracts of the country.

Hopeful Beginnings

In the beginnings in the late 1970s, Shining Path's founders were regarded in quite another light. The schism party that became popularly known as Shining Path grew out of the Maoist Peruvian Communist Party-*Bandera Roja* (Red Flag), founded by Arequipa-born philosophy professor, Guzmán. At the University of San Cristóbal de Huamanga, in Ayacucho in the central sierra, the group of intellectuals who formed around Guzmán were known as the *luminosos*.

Guzmán's party looked to Mao and China for its inspiration, seeing similarities between the peasants' revolutionary role in the Chinese revolution and the one that the tiny Peruvian group sought to ignite in this Andean city. The leader also drew inspiration from the writings of Mariátegui, who had seen in communal Andean organization a base for socialism. Yet Guzmán's closest allies were clearly from the elite of the city. Typical of these was Osman Morote, from an intellectual and landed family of *hacendados*, who was considered Guzmán's number two when captured in 1988. The hierarchical structure of the party, especially after it became a military machine, and the discipline demanded of members meant that power remained in the hands of Guzmán and his inner circle, which included some original members, until 1992.

From 1975, this group of mainly students and academics began to work in the countryside to garner support for its revolutionary teaching. In 1980 Guzmán decided it was time to put revolutionary theory into practice, and some of the members went underground.

The Armed Struggle

When five youths broke into the electoral registration center in Chuschi, a remote village in Ayacucho, and burned the ballot boxes on May 17, 1980, the start of Shining Path's insurgency passed virtually unnoticed. Ironically, it was the first day under democracy after twelve years of military rule.

By the end of that year, following some 100 attacks or disruptions, it had become clear that this was not a one-off protest. The Lima government of Belaúnde was slow to act against the movement in the far-off Andes. Initially, young *campesinos* seeking a better life and students in Ayacucho and Lima's state universities were keen recruits. At first, local people were tolerant of the group, which brought both revolutionary hopes and order by imposing a stern moral code which it imposed in the areas where it was active, punishing adulterers, wife-beaters, and thieves. These early years were typified by the funeral of a student, Edith Lagos, a Shining Path fighter killed in a clash with troops in Andahuaylas. Lagos had been a top student and a poet and was the daughter of a wealthy merchant in the city of Ayacucho. Thousands turned out for her funeral in September 1982, showing if not sympathy for Shining Path, at least tolerance of its presence.

Lagos was just one of Shining Path's many women leaders and militants. Women from all classes formed a crucial part of the movement. Among those imprisoned for Shining Path membership were a dancer from Lima high society, Maritza Garrido Lecca, and the Chilean wife of author José María Arguedas, Sybila Arredondo.

Even though people grew disillusioned with Shining Path as deaths mounted, the harsh repression which followed alienated many people from the government forces. The forces were ordered in by December 1982 after growing attacks finally provoked Belaúnde to declare an emergency and he became determined to eradicate the rebels at all costs. In the dirty war that ensued thousands died and thousands more were "disappeared." The military are believed to be responsible for half of the approximately 30,000 deaths from political violence in Peru between 1980 and 1997. While Shining Path ruthlessly killed scores of local authorities, peasant group leaders, or anyone they considered an agent of the state or a rival, including development workers, nuns, and priests, the military retaliated by unleashing similar brutality against the *campesinos*. The villagers' most common phrase for that period is to describe themselves as "caught in the crossfire." Roving Shining Path fighters would pass through their village and demand food. In their wake would come the military, who would shoot villagers for collaborating with Shining Path. Or vice versa.

Apart from the massacres which took place in these remote places, villagers also found the structure of their society disintegrating. Faced with Shining Path threats, mayors and other local officials resigned all over rural Peru, leaving large parts of the country without any civilian representatives. The insurgency spread to Lima, taking root in the shanty towns and among students, particularly at three state universities. Shining

Path's policy of goading the people and the government with acts of singular brutality succeeded in many places in installing anarchy and war. The military was equally feared; the massacre of 39 adults and 23 children in the village of Accomarca in 1995 was just one of many documented mass killings carried out by the security forces who seemed determined to take no prisoners.

Throughout the 1980s and into the 1990s the violence escalated, with new atrocities fanning the bitterness and fear. In 1986, protests by Shining Path inmates at three prisons in Lima were put down by the military with measures including aerial bombings. Human rights groups said that of the 124 prisoners killed in Lurigancho prison, around 100 were summarily executed. In July 1992, the bombing of the Tarata Street apartment block in the heart of Miraflores, a smart residential district of the capital, killed twenty people and wounded 132 others. The bomb attack against civilians set off a wave of deep revulsion against Shining Path in a city already worn down by the constant bombings, violent strikes, and blackouts.

Before the capture of Guzmán there were signs that the tide had turned. Shining Path's belief that it was the only group which could lead a revolution and its war on all other grassroots organizations had gained it countless enemies. It killed many trade unionists, peasant leaders, and local government officials. The killing in February 1992 of Maria Elena Moyano, the deputy mayor of Villa El Salvador, who had dared to speak out against Shining Path, crystallized the feeling that Shining Path did not take "the people" into account. In the countryside, the peasant self-defense groups or *rondas*, first imposed by the army, were beginning to act as a voluntary force to push Shining Path out.

When Guzmán was captured along with several other key leaders, the whole hierarchical organization began to cave in. The strange episode in which Guzmán asked from prison for a peace accord with the government, which was engineered by the intelligence service, split what remained of the rebel movement, which at its peak was considered to have had 5,000 members and a considerable number of sympathizers. Most of those who still followed Guzmán stopped fighting.

Shining Path has not disappeared. A "red" or hard-line rump led by "Feliciano," Oscar Ramírez Durand, has from time to time attacked with car bombs or shootings and so far the leader has evaded capture. He is said to be hiding with a small band of fighters in the inaccessible high jungle of Ayacucho. Analysts have reported that Shining Path also has active members in the north and in the jungle but that they have changed tack from their traditional methods. Analyst Carlos Tapia said that in 1996 Shining Path was starting to acknowledge that its indiscriminate killings of *campesinos* was a mistake, a revelation for a dogmatic organization which has seldom showed mercy or repentance, and that members were engaged more in recruiting new members and rebuilding the shattered movement, particularly in Lima's shanty towns, than in staging armed attacks.

A Long Hangover

To most Peruvians, it now seems incredible that Shining Path ever came so close to victory. Its successes owed much to the ability of Guzmán, who proved a consummate military tactician, developing a highly disciplined and secretive group organized in a honeycomb of tiny cells. Any captured member could generally only turn in a handful of other rebels. Guzmán found in the Andes the ideal context for the classic tactics of guerrilla movements which know the territory well, shift from place to place, and use surprise and fear to sow havoc. Guzmán also instilled in his followers an utter ruthlessness.

Among the many consequences of the Shining Path years which Peru has yet to confront is the virtual impunity given to a military which committed many atrocities. An amnesty law passed in June 1995, protecting any military operative involved in human rights abuses since 1980 from prosecution, freed the members of a death squad of intelligence agents who had kidnapped and killed nine students and a professor in 1992, practically the only charge against the military to get to court. The power of the security forces to intimidate, torture, and even kill was boosted during these years.

Equally, the imprisonment of hundreds of innocent people on terrorism charges in the disdain for human rights which has prevailed among some sectors of the military under the Fujimori government is only gradually being rectified. Under pressure from human rights groups, Fujimori set up a special commission to review terrorism cases and by mid-1997 had pardoned more than 100 prisoners. Yet rights groups consider several hundred more among some 4,000 such prisoners to have been wrongly imprisoned. Despite these miscarriages of justice, the military courts which sentenced the "innocents" continue to wield uncommonly wide powers over what most people would consider civilian cases.

Trouble and Strife

In his personal life Fujimori appears to be as cold-blooded as in politics. After Fujimori's wife, Susana Higuchi, also of Japanese descent, began to accuse some members of her husband's family of corruption, including selling off clothes that were intended as charitable donations, she was slowly shut out of the presidential circle. Higuchi claims to have been treated maliciously, going so far as to claim that intelligence agents tried to poison her by sending noxious gases through the palace air-conditioning. Whatever the truth, the relationship was clearly over.

As divorce proceedings began, Higuchi tried to fight back and put herself forward as a candidate for the 1995 presidential elections to run against her husband. The electoral board threw out her candidacy, claiming that she had not enough supporting signatures. When the board subsequently barred her from standing for Congress, saying her party list was incomplete, Higuchi went on hunger strike on the sidewalk outside. With her lips parched from the heat and barely able to speak, Higuchi cut a pathetic figure and was soon taken to a clinic to recover. This meant that she never tested a law conveniently passed by Congress, prohibiting immediate members of the president's family from presenting presidential candidacies, which the press dubbed the "Susana law" since its intention was clearly to stop her. The presidential couple eventually ended their relationship with a fairly quiet divorce. Her claims that Fujimori banned their children from visiting her seem not to be entirely true, but there is no doubt that the four children spend far more time with their father than their mother who has clearly come out of the affair physically weakened and psychologically the loser. When analysts seek to describe Fujimori's ruthlessness they say, "Just look what happened to his wife ..."

After his political grouping penned a new constitution permitting immediate presidential re-election, Fujimori was returned as president in 1995 with 64 per cent of valid votes in elections which international observers judged to be generally free and fair. Not only did his easy victory over former UN secretary-general Javier Perez de Cuellar restore Fujimori's debatable political legitimacy, but the president's rise was completed by the annihilation of the traditional political parties, most of which failed to get even the five per cent of votes needed to register as a party. Winning 67 out of 120 congressional seats, Fujimori's Cambio 90 won a comfortable majority, leaving the once-mighty APRA with a mere eight seats.

Although he clearly answers a need in war-battered Peruvians for order, Fujimori's style of leadership is not as modern and unique as he likes to portray it. In many ways, his reliance on the military and an expanded intelligence service for power and information harks back to a long-standing tradition in which the military has never been far from power. The key figure in his entourage is a cashiered army captain-turned-lawyer, Vladimiro Montesinos, who has risen to become the chief of the intelligence service. The balding, bespectacled Montesinos could be considered Fujimori's alter ego, reflecting the darker side of his character. The adviser has been accused of masterminding the Colina Group, a paramilitary death squad responsible for the killings of people at a party in the central Lima district of Barrios Altos and of nine students and a professor kidnapped from La Cantuta university. Despite accusations, Montesinos has never been charged in the case against the La Cantuta killers, nor as a result of a top drug-trafficker's accusations that he took pay-offs in return for protecting his drug ring. A television station in 1997 revealed that Montesinos was earning $70,000 a month, apparently from his private legal practice, stirring suspicions of influence-peddling.

With the passing of a law that would ostensibly allow Fujimori to stand for a third term in 2000, Peruvians will face a choice between re-electing one of Latin America's most durable presidents or gambling on another leader who might undo the stability which the strong-armed Fujimori administration has delivered. With the rout of the old parties in the early 1990s, no clear opponent has yet emerged. New movements are likely to be personality-based, since Peruvians remain shy of anything which smacks of ideology. Contenders will have to take on not only Fujimori, but also the military machine which has practically co-existed in power with him.

Meanwhile, there has been no significant shift of wealth to the poor, who still make up half the population, and power in Peru remains highly concentrated, not just in the executive government, but in one man. It is no coincidence that the favorite teaser in intellectual circles is, "What would happen if Fujimori's plane crashed?" The answer, it seems, is, "Anything."

The Túpac Amaru Rebels

Since taking up arms in 1984, the Túpac Amaru Revolutionary Movement (MRTA) has lived in the shadow of the larger, more hostile Shining Path. This pro-Cuban movement was cast in the mold of left-wing guerrilla movements which had sprung up all over the region. The MRTA established a network of contacts with other rebel groups in Chile, Colombia, and elsewhere which it later used for arms supplies and to concoct plans for a never-realized revolution across Latin America. The main difference between the MRTA and Shining Path was that the former, which grew out of a collection of tiny far-left parties, sought to work side by side with other grassroots organizations. Shining Path saw all these, including the MRTA, as "revisionists" and enemies.

Led by Victor Polay, a left-winger who in his student days had been a close friend of former president Alan García, the MRTA established strongholds in the northern jungle department of San Martín, including the central Huallaga valley, Junin department in central Peru, and alongside Shining Path on the campuses of the more radical state universities. Its troops, wearing combat fatigues, courted publicity. It favored grand gestures, as in the takeover of the town of Juanjui in 1987, when the MRTA invited in the press to televise a military attack which turned into a jamboree with the rebels organizing soccer matches and dances with the locals.

The rebels' favorite targets were bank branches or buildings connected to hated "imperialists" like the USA and Japan, with attacks on such places as the Kentucky Fried Chicken fast-food chain. Rebels frequently took over international news agency offices in Lima, leaving behind revolutionary graffiti and trying to force the transmission of their messages. The MRTA also made Robin Hood gestures with the ransacking of Lima supermarkets to give out food in shanty towns, or hijacked cargo trucks carrying Coca-Cola or food and divided out the spoils on the spot.

Increasingly, however, the group focused on more lucrative operations like kidnapping top business leaders or extorting industrialists and drug traffickers. Kidnap victims, like television magnate Héctor Delgado Parker, were kept in so-called people's prisons, tiny cells dug into the floor. In most cases, hostages were ransomed, but sometimes the hostage was killed. Although experts consider the MRTA responsible for a small fraction of total deaths from political violence from 1980 onwards, the group resorted to some brutal killings of its own members as internal feuds broke out from time to time.

By 1996, the MRTA was rarely heard of in the capital. Like Shining Path, it was weakened by tougher anti-terrorist laws, a law of repentance that obliged those who turned themselves in to denounce other rebels, and the capture of many leaders. In December that year, a shoot-out at the group's main Lima safe house in the respectable district of La Molina came as a shock. Among those captured were the group's number two, Miguel Rincón, and a 26-year-old New Yorker, Lori Berenson, who was accused of being a link in the group's arms chain and helping to plan an attack on Congress, foiled by the swoop. The arrests of the La Molina group led many to believe that MRTA was virtually dismantled. At most it had a couple of hundred fighters holed up in the jungle.

Ironically, when the authorities had announced the virtual disappearance of the MRTA, it pulled off its most dramatic attack. The world suddenly discovered the group when thirteen rebels, led by former trade union leader Nestor Cerpa, blasted their way into the Japanese ambassador's residence in Lima during an elegant reception, taking hundreds of hostages. Cerpa publicly insisted that he would accept nothing less in the way of a settlement than 400 of his comrades freed from jail. Fujimori pledged that he would not release a single terrorist.

Finally, on April 22, 1997, the siege ended as dramatically as it began. As the rebels played football, commandos blasted their way into the residence through a network of tunnels dug over the four months. Amid thick smoke spirals and a chain of explosions, the hostages were guided out. Seventy-one of the 72 hostages were rescued alive. Two commandos and all fourteen rebels died. Some hostages reported that the troops executed some of the rebels as they tried to surrender.

40

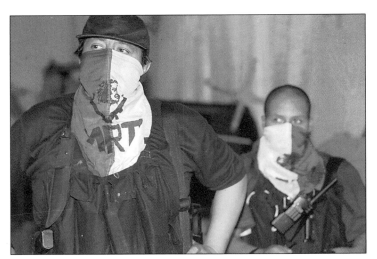

Nestor Cerpa and comrade at a press conference during the siege.

Sengo Pérez/Reportage

The death of Cerpa has undoubtedly left the already weak group reeling, particularly as he was a founder member and one of the few surviving veterans. The attack was dismissed by the government as an "isolated incident," while experts like Carlos Iván Degregori described the guerrillas as an anachronism in the last chapter of a story which had already finished.

One lesson of the residence siege is clear, however. As long as there are a few well-armed and determined rebels left in Peru, there is a chance of a repeat operation. Cerpa's last stand focused attention on the jungle area where his recruits came from, where a cycle of poverty offers youngsters little hope of a better life. As some of the hostages themselves admitted, these areas of deprivation and exclusion require urgent attention if governments wish to lay the ghost of Túpac Amaru.

Democracy

Cynics are fond of remarking that Peruvians have no idea of democracy. It is true that full parliamentary democracy is still young in Peru, since it was only in 1979 that all adult Peruvians were given the vote when the literacy qualification was removed. Ingrained traditions of military interference and *caudillo* populism have also obstructed the development of a democratic political culture, while recent experiences of civil war and terrorism have encouraged popular support for authoritarian rule.

Yet if electoral democracy is fragile, other forms of communal and democratic decision-making have stronger roots in Peru. The notion of community, in particular, is an ancient value among Peruvians, who in the Inca period were organized in communal units or *ayllus*, which still exist in some rural areas. Many surviving Andean communities continue to be structured along age-old lines of shared responsibility, and villagers still get together to carry out communal tasks, like repairing irrigation, house-building, or harvesting, always accompanied by the fiesta atmosphere that takes hold whenever Peruvians get together.

The move to the cities has brought out a strong individualistic streak in migrants, who perhaps have no option but to be self-starters, with thousands of informal-sector traders working alone in a situation of cut-throat competition. However, the Andean tradition of *aynis* (community work) has been revived even in the shanty towns of Lima, such as in El Agustino, for instance, where residents worked every Sunday to build a railway line. Peruvians make sharing a part of festivities and beer or *chicha* is drunk in a circle, with a single glass making the round again and again.

Shared responsibility and solidarity are evident in rural villages and modern shanty towns, particularly among women. The most common local organizations are the thousands of *comedores populares* or soup kitchens, where families pool their resources to cook more cheaply. Similar community initiatives include the *vaso de leche* ("glass of milk") programs which distribute contributed milk and breakfast foods to local children; and *wawa wasis*, a cheaper version of child care centers where women take turns to care for each other's children. Housing, too, is organized communally, from the basic *asentamientos humanos* among the poor to the fancier *urbanizaciones* of the middle and upper classes. This collective effort makes it easier to press for land titles and the installation of water and electricity. At weekends, music blares out on streets of shanty towns where families or organizations are holding fund-raising parties where food and drink is sold at a tiny profit. People go along to help their neighbors and expect help in their turn.

Democracy has taken on a new meaning under Fujimori, who claims to have put into action "direct democracy," a dialogue between the leader and his people, with no intermediaries except perhaps the television screens seen in four million homes. As Fujimori prefers to work idiosyncratically in random and well-publicized visits to shanty towns and rural areas, there appears little that is lasting about his personal version of democracy. An engineer by training, Fujimori prefers to consider himself as the technocratic manager of a company called Peru. A few institutions like Foro Democrático have tried to encourage new civic groups to emerge as a counterbalance to presidential power and to take up wider social concerns, such as strengthening the weak judicial system. So far, however, dynamic new representatives of Peruvian civil society have been slow in appearing.

3   ECONOMY: GIFT OF THE DEVIL

At a rural market high in the Andes, lines of *campesinos* squat beside their produce spread on blankets on the ground. Most wait patiently, chewing coca leaves. In the most remote markets of the highlands and jungle, money is not strictly necessary. Peasants still exchange potatoes and corn for cooking oil and pasta in an age-old system of barter known as *trueque*.

Watching the trading floor at New York's stock exchange in July 1996, then Peruvian Presidency Minister Jaime Yoshiyama breaks out in a broad grin as the orange-light ticker flashes up the message "Welcome to Telefónica del Perú." The government had just sold off most of its remaining stake in the country's old telephone monopoly to international trading houses in a hugely over-subscribed offer. Telefónica del Perú is trading high on Wall Street.

A bank executive is driving to work in Lima, talking on his cellular phone. As he draws up at the traffic lights of a busy road, he can see a procession of street traders filing past. An old lady, with flowers in her hat, taps the window and thrusts out a dirty cup. Men pass quickly with notices hung around their necks saying, "Calculators, 5 soles." Others hang in at the car window to offer bananas, candy, sunglasses, live lizards, electric cables or newspapers. Young women with huge yellow coolbags clutch fistfuls of ice creams. A scruffy child tries to wipe the car windshield with a dirty green cloth. The lights change and the banker drives on to the office.

As Peru hurtles back into the mainstream of international financial markets, its economy continues to straddle a deep divide among different regions, different classes and what can even seem like different centuries. Economic recovery since 1992 has, if anything, deepened the gap between rich and poor, between the subsistence lifestyle of the rural small farmer or street hawker and that of the modern financial and industrial sector.

Peru's Wealth

Peru's natural bounty should make it the envy of other nations. It has vast mineral resources in gold, silver, copper, zinc, lead, and iron, and extensive deposits of oil and natural gas lying under its surface. Its unusually cold seas swarm with fish, attracting flocks of birds, which leave behind the guano which was so highly prized in the nineteenth century. Almost anything grows in Peru, where the variety of soils, altitudes, and climates produces a multitude of agricultural commodities, ranging from *ají* and potatoes in the sierra, coffee, cocoa, and coca in the *ceja de selva*, to cotton,

Preparing potatoes for storage   *Toribio Mendoza/TAFOS*

sugar-cane, and "non-traditionals" like asparagus and broccoli in the coastal sun.

Yet Peru's roller-coaster economic history suggests that these natural assets have been, in the words of economist Rosemary Thorp, "a gift of the devil," and the devil has been more than generous to Peru. Gold, guano, copper, sugar, rubber, oil, wool, minerals, and fishmeal have each taken a turn at spurring a jump in foreign earnings for Peru. The boom in each commodity has come in short, sharp bursts, dictated by international markets and global prices. Each has brought short-term benefits, like the building of Peru's railways with guano wealth, but none has led to long-term and sustainable development for the majority of Peruvians. As Thorp observes, "From the very onset of colonial rule, rich natural resources have indirectly led to distorted political, social, and economic structures."

The availability of primary products has through the years favored foreign investors and debt markets and made the country too dependent on imports. It has also distracted attention from the needs of languishing sierra agriculture and the growing mass of urban poor. When natural resources have been in Peruvian hands, such as during the state ownership of the guano industry in the nineteenth century, these have often been used frivolously to pay for luxury imports or have generated extravagant spending on infrastructure of limited economic benefit, like the railways. The illusion of prosperity has led to borrowing and debt beyond Peru's means. Otherwise, export profits have more often been in foreign hands, with little reinvested in the country.

Peruvian governments have also found it difficult to reach a compromise in their relationship with foreign investors, swerving between over-generous incentives and draconian sanctions, as when General Velasco nationalized the oil industry without paying compensation. Many of Peru's key industries have been developed by foreign companies, like the Cerro de Pasco mining company, the W.R. Grace company in sugar and agri-exports, and the International Petroleum Corporation in the northern oil fields. The vice-president of Citibank could rightly claim in 1927 that, "The vast majority of the principal sources of wealth in Peru ... are controlled by foreign owners, and apart from wages and taxes, none of the value of production is retained in the country." Most foreign corporations active in the Peruvian economy have been U.S.-based, although British and Canadian firms have operated through local subsidiaries.

It was not until the development of manufacturing industry on the central coast in the 1950s and the emergence of mostly locally-owned fishmeal plants in the 1960s that a Peruvian industrial class began playing a significant role. But this new focus of local wealth was not enough to right the deep divisions which marked Peru, with the majority of people, the urban poor and rural *campesinos*, left behind.

Exports and Imports

Peru remains a country dependent for its economic prospects on the health of its export earnings, and its main exchange-earners are minerals, particularly copper, iron, silver, and gold, and fishmeal. These traditional products are unlikely to lose their weight in Peru's export income in the near future. With strong investment in the mining sector and the widest ever coverage of the country with mining claims, analysts predict a sharp upswing in export earnings at the end of the century which will help right the balance-of-payments deficit. The dominant position of mining means that it will continue to account for at least three-quarters of Peru's export earnings until well past 2000. Peruvian exporters are pushing for a greater diversification of products sold abroad. The National Exporters Association cites booming sales of asparagus and cotton clothing, but traditional exports of raw materials continue to dwarf such new-comers.

The Yanacocha gold mine in the northern sierra state of Cajamarca is partly responsible for the mining fever simmering in Peru, which has recently become South America's biggest producer. On this mountain plain, a relatively new mining technique which can separate the gold using a cyanide solution is producing one of the highest returns in the industry. The U.S.-Peruvian consortium which owns most of the mine has costs of just over $100-an-ounce, half those of regional competitors. Yet Latin America's most productive gold mine looks almost abandoned, because so few people are directly employed in the high-tech process. Local people have some jobs moving waste on the site, but even including those involved in improving the roads to the mine and other spin-off social projects, this kind of mining offers scant hope for the unemployed.

Since colonial times when the Spanish hankered after European finery, Peru has shown a penchant for imported goods. From being Latin America's first oil producer, Peru now has an oil deficit of some $300 million each year, partly because most of its own crude oil is very heavy, forcing it to import more expensive, lighter crude oil for other products such as gasoline. If Shell decides to go ahead with its $3 billion project to develop the Camisea gas fields, this imbalance should be gradually reversed. Peru also meets a large part of its food needs with imports, particularly wheat and pasta. Successive campaigns to try to promote local produce or grains have been unable to rein in demand for these imports, which are now highly prized in the sierra and selva regions.

Stability and Credit

Economic stability since 1991 has put an end to rampant inflation. Moneychangers, sporting new green cloth jackets with their names and brash dollar signs, rarely bother to race one another to clients, but sit on sidewalk stools waiting for customers to pass. Margins are very thin, they say, now that the Peruvian sol is stable.

On both side of the *Zanjón* ("the big ditch"), as the expressway linking central Lima with the seaside suburbs of Miraflores and Barranco is known, motorists can see a line of ever-more daring, geometric office blocks built to house the new banks settling in the Peruvian capital. Construction sites are dotted around the capital. Hundreds of apartment blocks are taking over vacant lots or elbowing out peeling one-story houses. Megastores and new supermarkets are taking shape behind huge advertising hoardings. American-style fast-food hamburger, fried chicken, and video franchises seem to appear almost overnight in smarter districts of Lima, while teenagers have found a new pastime: hanging out at the shiny, 24-hour gas-and-shopping stations that have replaced rickety old roadside pumps. Sleek new cars with Asian trademarks snake their way through the clogged traffic, edging by aging Volkswagen Beetles, which until recently ruled Lima roads.

Signs of economic renewal are evident in the capital. After almost 30 years in which few Peruvians had any chance of a personal loan, banks are now competing to offer the fastest, cheapest mortgages or loans to buy a car, a television, a vacation, or to pay school fees. Consumer credit has

Banks in Miraflores   *Tony Morrison/South American Pictures*

arrived, even if interest rates are more than double what consumers expect in Europe or North America.

Economic Medicine

The buzz in the capital's up-market financial and shopping districts is the visible result of the drastic overhaul of the Peruvian economy underway since 1990. When Fujimori took over the government that year, the outlook was bleak, with no foreign currency in the Central Bank coffers and inflation reaching a delirious 7,650 per cent. Foreign lenders had cut off credit to Peru, and local industrialists and foreign investors alike were pulling out as rebel violence spread to the capital, bringing bomb attacks on bank branches, kidnappings and extortion. As Alán García left the presidency, the state sector had reached unprecedented levels of bankruptcy, its workforce swollen by years of patronage and corruption.

The new president, with neo-liberal Economy Minister Carlos Boloña, took drastic steps. With advice from the international financial institutions, they introduced a classic shock program, trying to bring the economy back from the brink. They put a stop to the *maquinita*, the printing of currency that was the resort of previous governments, anchoring a new currency, the sol, against real reserves and income. Prices and currency exchange rates were freed to find their real market rate. They vowed to slash the public sector payroll and privatize all state-owned companies in what was one of the most radical plans in Latin America. Tariffs on imports were cut. The stock market was privatized and given autonomy. Lima made overtures to its international creditors to start talking about restructuring its foreign debt.

The immediate results of "Fujishock" were harsh for many. Economists began talking about the new poor, as some 200,000 workers were laid off from the state sector. In the shanty towns, soup kitchens became a part of life. Many local factories, long used to preferential market treatment, went to the wall as import barriers fell and cheaper foreign-made products filled the market.

Privatization

The atmosphere in the hall of the gigantic Museo de la Nación on February 28, 1994 was taut with nerves, although the businessmen arriving in dark suits tried to show otherwise, greeting one another with hearty backslapping and firm handshakes, before filing into the packed rows. When the consortium led by the Spanish company, Telefónica announced its bid for the 35 per cent stake of the Peruvian telephone companies which would give it management control, there was a momentary stunned intake of breath around the room, followed by thunderous applause. The offer of $2 billion was more than double the next-highest bid and four times above the reserve price.

The Telefónica sale heralded a new mood and was a huge success for Peru's privatization program. In 1993 and 1994 the economy romped ahead; the growth rate of 12.8 per cent in 1994 was the highest in the world. Inflation settled down close to single figures. A radical privatization program which by April 1997 had sold dozens of companies and raised $7.1 billion finally met with little resistance, apart from the dispute which delayed the break-up of state oil company, Petroperú.

Yet the runaway boom which put Fujimori, portrayed in a Superman outfit, on the cover of market-wise financial magazines like *Latin Trade* did not last for long. An electoral spending spree in 1994-5 which saw the president pour out funds on building schools, roads and housing projects soon had the country straying from the path of neo-liberal doctrine. Money lenders like the International Monetary Fund that had agreed economic goals with Peru voiced their concern. The current account deficit ran up above seven per cent, setting alarm bells ringing in the wake of the Mexican currency slide. Peru's government had no choice but to slam on the brakes, and spending stopped almost dead. Economic growth in 1996 was just 2.8 per cent. With population growth still at around 1.8 per cent annually, it was as though the country had been treading water. Recovery started again immediately but was expected to be deliberately slow and steady. The sharp advances made against poverty between 1991 and 1995, when the number of poor fell to 45.3 per cent, from 55 per cent, also halted. By 1997, poverty was at best standing still.

Although Peru's return to the neo-liberal recipe has been encouraged and welcomed in New York and Tokyo, where Lima is hailed as a prodigal son, the vigor with which the country has slashed the state's role and protections for its domestic producers is now being questioned at home. A feeling is growing that the reforms which brought stability might have gone too far, too fast. Even the government, which has raised its social spending to 40 per cent of the budget, is now talking about "ultra-liberalism" in the modern sectors of the economy, but something closer to "socialism" in the country's poorer areas. Isolated interventionist measures such as tinkering with customs duties on food imports and offering tax breaks to some industrialists and within selected geographic areas look set to increase as countries throughout the region retreat from radical neo-liberalism to construct some protection for their weakest economic sectors.

Agriculture

Peru's agricultural sector, ranging from modern agro-industry to scrubland subsistence plots, is one key to the country's economic dilemma. Before agrarian reform, the old highland estates were run by an elite of landowners, who had pushed most of the free Indian communities on to the poorest land of the bare *puna*, and ran their estates like fiefdoms. Farming methods even on the estates were often backward and productivity was low. The old-fashioned *haciendas* contrasted with large coastal estates in irrigated river valleys, which were run as big business. Productivity was high, and cotton and sugar were responsible for export earnings from which several Peruvian and foreign families, like the Romeros, later built up diversified business empires.

Land reform under Velasco did not solve the problems of the rural sector. Although it destroyed the power of the sierra elite and turned the large coastal estates over to workers, there had been no planning and scant technical assistance to turn them into managers. Assets were generally sold off for a pittance, while productivity fell further, with little modernization of farming methods. One example was the sugar cooperatives, where sugar production slumped from a peak of a million tons a year to barely half that.

Despite the massive migration of the 1970s and 1980s, the recovery of the rural sector remains overdue. More than 30 per cent of Peruvians still work in agriculture, and statistics for the poorest rural populations are sadly similar to those of sub-Saharan Africa. In Huancavelica, the child mortality rate is 130 per 1,000 births, nearly three times the average in Lima, while life expectancy averages 51 years, compared to 72 years in the capital. Two-thirds of the country's "extreme" poor live in rural areas.

While the agricultural sector has been growing since 1993, the expansion has been confined to the larger agro-industrial estates which have benefited from Fujimori's relaxation of previously strict landholding limits. The sharecroppers on the coast and *campesino* communities in the sierra, meanwhile, are struggling just to maintain their subsistence lifestyle and in many cases cannot even afford to buy seed. For highland farmers, one of the greatest problems remains credit, especially since the recent abolition of the development banks has cut off the means of buying seed or eking out the long period between sowing and harvest. Programs of road-building and repairs introduced by the Fujimori government have helped, but many

Coca in the market place   *Annie Bungeroth*

farmers have been unable to sow crops and in some cases have been forced to reduce planting. The government's delay in settling the long-running problem of the ownership of water supplies with a new water law has also hampered the development of poorer farming sectors.

Coca

Coca is one response to rural poverty. Ash-green, crackly coca leaves were sacred in Inca times and have been grown since time immemorial in Peru. *Campesinos* in the Andes still chew wads of coca leaves to fight off tiredness and hunger and use them in ritual prayers, while folk-healers read the future from the way the leaves fall from their hands.

The rise in U.S. demand for cocaine, made from coca leaf, spurred coca-growing on the eastern slopes of the Andes in the 1960s, mainly in the Huallaga valley in the north. Coca was everything that legal crops like coffee and cocoa were not. Small farmers did not have to worry about roads to market, since the market, mostly in the form of Colombian drug-runners, came to them and paid cash on the nail. The coca trade came complete with its own infrastructure. It arrived in the normally remote *ceja de selva* area as a trail of small planes flown in from across the border. The crop was also a quick and regular moneymaker, since it yielded a harvest up to six times a year and was easy to tend. There was, however, a major drawback: while coca cultivation was not in itself illegal, it was the first step in an illegal trade. But the high returns not only led farmers to turn a blind eye, but also attracted new migrants to the area to take part in the boom.

Attempts to stamp out coca-growing, backed by the U.S. government, had the opposite effect. A clamp-down in the Alto Huallaga area simply spread the coca fields from a small area to the length of the eastern spine of the Andes. In all, the area where coca could potentially be grown was 150,000 square miles, an area too large to be effectively policed, particularly with available resources. Coca-growing was soon out of control.

Peru in the 1980s became the world's largest producer of coca leaf, accounting for around 60 per cent of the crop. In the coca-growing areas, the drug mafias effectively took over, creating a frontier culture of luxury goods and shotgun justice. Peru's greatest headache was not the trade, estimated to be worth between $650 million and $1 billion at its peak in early 1994, but the unholy alliance which sprang up between the coca-growing areas and the country's two main guerrilla groups, the Shining Path and the MRTA. "Fees" for protecting coca growers or for granting permission for planes to land were quickly making the Peruvian rebels rich. The government from 1992 hit on what it considered was the only viable strategy. It confirmed that coca-growing was not illegal, lifting any threat of reprisals from the 200,000 families who lived off the trade, and put the area under army control. The army's brief was to target the rebels, not the coca growers, and to try to cut the guerrillas out of the drug business. Lima journalists have cited several cases of drug bands paying the army instead of the rebels to allow drug lifts, and it appears that some level of corruption was tolerated as a lesser evil.

But soon, in common with so many of Peru's raw material booms, circumstances abroad determined a decline in the commodity's profitability. The clamp-down in Colombia on the Cali cartel closed the market for a while and stifled demand. Prices slumped from heyday prices of $60 an *arroba* (25lbs) to $5 for the same amount. With demand for the drug stable in the main markets, another development hit the Peruvian small farmer, as Colombia started growing coca for itself. With techniques tried and tested in Peru, some experts claimed that production in Colombia had by 1997 surpassed that in Peru. Although there were signs that Peru had progressed to manufacturing coca into the finished cocaine, local mafias were still small-time compared to those of Colombia or Mexico.

The fall in the price of coca seems unlikely to lead to the elimination of the crop, at least in the short term. Outside the Huallaga valley, where the economy revolves around coca, the plots, generally tended by families with crops in both the sierra and the *ceja de selva*, can be left to grow with

little attention, waiting for a possible improvement in this volatile market. Although these farming families have probably lost around twenty per cent of their income because of coca's decline, there is little acute hardship since family production and income are usually diversified to include potatoes, corn, coffee, and other crops. Apart from some increase in rural poverty, however, one of the slump's damaging side effects has been the increased availability and cheapness of highly-addictive coca paste in Peru. Drug addiction, once minimal, is now a growing problem among poorer city dwellers. The more expensive cocaine is also considered part of a night out for the racier set among the rich.

Boys working in
Lima's fruit market   *Susana Pastor/TAFOS*

Employment and the Informal Sector

If asked, most Peruvians would probably say that their greatest problem, especially since 1993, has been finding employment. Yet, paradoxically, it is hard to find a Peruvian who does not work. There is no social security net, except perhaps for a free meal at a soup kitchen, for those who earn nothing. The vast majority of the poor have no choice but to work in jobs which pay little and offer no security. As one government adviser admits, "Our problem is not one of jobs, but one of income." Official figures show how far the standard of living has fallen. Wages in 1994 were worth 43.3 per cent of what they were in 1987, recovering from 1990 when they had tumbled to 31.1 per cent of levels three years earlier.

Huge numbers of underemployed people are hidden among the crowds who hawk a living selling goods or services on the street. The sheer variety of items on offer testifies both to the scale of the problem and to the ingenuity of a people who dream up a thousand ways to get by. You can get a street haircut, have torn clothes sewn up by a sidewalk sewing machine, as well as using the services of the more traditional shoe-shiners and car-washers. Others stand by bus stops recording the time at which vehicles from different bus lines pass. For their market information, the highly competitive *combi* drivers give them a few cents.

Some analysts, notably Hernando de Soto in his classic neo-liberal work, *The Other Path*, have argued that by harnessing this creativity and breaking down the state's red tape, the country would have a dynamic future. The reality is, however, that creative production is limited and most of the street sellers are simply middlemen, buying and selling at tiny profits.

hese subsistence workers are lumped by statistics into the amorphous "informal" sector, which includes all those who have no contract or legal work existence in the country's huge paperless economy. The International Labor Organization estimates that 54 per cent of Lima workers have no contract or formal job. Half of these, around 800,000 adults plus innumerable children, work on the street. Yet cold statistics paint an inaccurate picture of what is going on, partly because the very nature of so much informality is that it is clandestine. According to the figures, around ten per cent of the labor force is openly unemployed, rising to 25 per cent among youths. In 1995, 46.1 per cent were working in the so-called modern sector, with a legal contract, and 53.9 per cent in the precarious informal sector.

Another confusing factor is that most Peruvians, even the most highly-qualified, have several jobs. Teachers and nurses top up their wages with fund-raising parties, selling food or goods like jewelry and clothes, often during working hours. Many professional workers spend their spare time using their car as a taxi, a major source of informal income which merely requires a handwritten note in the window saying "Taxi." Those with some savings may rent out taxi fleets or minibuses. It is no surprise, therefore, that Peru has one of the lowest productivity rates in Latin America.

Determining how many people earn a living wage is very difficult, particularly as the state "minimum wage" of just over $100-a-month is hardly enough to support one person, much less a family. Apart from poverty statistics, which estimate that around 49 per cent of Peruvians are living below the poverty line, unable to satisfy their basic needs, there is no exact measure of what average Peruvians actually earn. What is clear is that Peru is lagging behind most of Latin America.

In Peru, as in most of the region, the employment situation in general is getting progressively worse. Slackening of labor laws makes it far easier to lay off workers, give short-term contracts or farm out work to "service agencies," which provide cheap labor with a minimum of employer obligation. The take-home pay of a youth stacking supermarket shelves for twelve hours a day is about 10 soles ($3.83) daily. Lack of jobs means that young people are lining up for this kind of work.

Economic Power

Wealth and power over the economy remains highly concentrated in Peru. The country has always had a tiny, dominant economic elite, although its membership has varied over the past three centuries. In the 1980s, it was the so-called "Twelve Apostles" who controlled the country's main private-sector activities as family-based conglomerates, combining financial services with real estate and other industries. The twelve were so powerful and identifiable that they formed an advisory committee to former president García. Although they later fell out with the president, most big business in that period reaped significant rewards from his policy of encouraging domestic industries with subsidies and incentives.

New investment in mining and oil and gas, together with privatization, has swung the pendulum away from the local groups towards foreign owners like Spain's Telefónica, China's iron-producing Shougang Corporation, and Spanish and Chilean banks. However, most of the Twelve Apostles are adapting to the new situation by forming coalitions with foreign capital and taking up minority stakes in telecommunications and other interests, providing the "know-whom" in the old-boy network of the Lima market. Interest on capital which is far higher than in more stable markets means that those with capital can hardly help making more.

Some of the Apostles, like Backus and Johnston, retain an almost monopolistic grasp on their key sectors, in this case, brewing. Others, like the Romero and Wiese banking families, are starting to feel the pressure from some foreign competition. On the whole, the traditional groups are seeking strategic partnerships with in-comers, shoring up their capital base by issuing international bonds and seeking foreign listings on Wall Street to make their financial position solid enough to survive.

Debt and Regional Markets

The agreement in March 1997 to restructure Peru's debt with its commercial creditors was hailed as ending thirteen years on the blacklist of the world's major banks. Although the accord will open up opportunities for fresh loans at more attractive interest rates, this must be handled carefully by a country as prone to busting its credit as Peru. Some economists protest, however, that the price paid by Peru was too high. Manuel Moreyra, a former Central Bank president, has pointed out that while creditors admitted in the late 1980s that they would be happy to get back five per cent of their capital, the 1997 deal ended up paying 130 per cent of the original debt. Whether or not Peru overpaid, the plan adds around $300 million a year to the debt-servicing bill which will reach \$1.6 billion annually, or more than 25 per cent of 1996 export earnings, rising to \$1.8 billion after 2002.

To keep pace Peru must push up production and earnings. As ever, the government is pinning its hopes on mining and hydrocarbons, led by the \$3 billion contract to exploit the Camisea gas fields. Primary products and foreign investment remain at the center of the government's plans for growth and recovery. Yet Moreyra is among those who say that what recovery has occurred is superficial, since it does not tackle the underlying structural problems of Peru: the gradual impoverishment of most Peruvians and a dependent economy geared to extracting natural resources, which places the highest value on raw materials and the lowest on people's work.

Growing trade links among the Latin American nations appear to offer the best chance of diversifying Peru's economy. Peru pulled out of the five-nation Andean Group in 1997, but has been actively seeking association with the dynamic Mercosur free-trade bloc, which, with Brazil and Argentina as leading members, is the most successful of the regional groupings. Opportunities in regional markets could give a boost to small and medium-sized enterprises, still starved of reasonably priced credit. Yet Peruvian manufacturers also fear that deregulated competition with powerful Brazilian and Argentine exporters could wipe out the few remaining domestic factories.

Beginning in 1998, Peru will also seek to emulate Chile, its role model in the region, by finding new Asian markets when it enters the Asia Pacific Economic Cooperation Forum, a mainly Asian trading bloc. There is little to suggest, however, that Peru can develop goods with greater added value to increase its return on exports, and everything indicates instead that it will mean more imported cars and electrical goods in return for Asian purchases of raw materials. Looking ahead, mining will remain the mainstay of export income, leaving Peru continually vulnerable to international market price swings.

4   SOCIETY AND PEOPLE: ALL THE BLOODS

Walk down the bustling central Lima pedestrian street, the Jirón de la Unión, and look into the sea of faces: the moneychangers, the street traders selling clothes, the shop assistants, the restaurant waiters, the stock market traders in ties on their lunch break, the policeman, the shoeshine boy, the beggar woman sitting with her hand held reverently outstretched. The spectrum of activities is mirrored in the variety of features. With migration from the highlands in recent years, Lima has become a more accurate reflection of all Peru's people.

Europeans and native Andeans, Afro-Peruvians, immigrant Chinese, Japanese, Italians, Germans, and, to a lesser extent, indigenous Amazon tribes, have mingled for so long that many Peruvians could fairly claim to have *todas las sangres* ("all the bloods"), the title of an influential novel by José Maria Arguedas, himself a *mestizo* of mixed European-Indian ancestry. Unlike some countries where people of different races lived strictly apart, unions between Europeans and Peruvian Andeans began from the moment the Spaniards arrived. Conquistador leader Francisco Pizarro lived with two royal Inca princesses and had four children. He acknowledged his paternity, even though he did not marry either of the mothers, both of whom went on to marry other Spaniards.

Centuries of immigration, migration, and intermarriage have continued the mix. Many Peruvians have ancestors from all the different ethnic groups. In the words of a popular song made famous by the gravel-voiced Afro-Peruvian musician, Zambo Cavero, "*El que no tiene de Inga, tiene de Mandinga*," meaning that the Peruvian who does not have some trace of *Inga* or Inca ancestors, has *Mandinga* or black ancestors. Frequently, he or she has a bit of both.

Discrimination

Despite the melting pot, Peruvians still have not come completely to terms with the fact that their country is one of Ingas and Mandingas. Although the feudal society of the *haciendas* has become part of the past, Peru is still battling against the hangover of the centuries in which the Spaniards subjugated indigenous Peruvians. Even after independence, Indians were held in *enganche* (hook) systems, virtual serfdoms, or lived in the deeply paternalistic society of the old haciendas where the landlord not only ran the local economy, but meted out justice too. Black slaves arrived with the Spanish, and when they were finally freed, Chinese immigrants were brought to work the land as laborers in similarly dismal conditions.

Pizarro, entertained on shore by a Peruvian lady

Peruvians' attitude to themselves is colored by this past. It is a society crisscrossed not only by its varied racial roots, but also by deep prejudices between rich and poor, and between those living in Lima and in the provinces. This prejudice survives despite the extent to which different communities have merged. Until recently, most television advertising contained almost exclusively white, European-type faces. Locally produced soap operas have generated a "brat pack" of young actors selected because they share a similar look, with blue or green eyes and blond hair, the opposite of indigenous Peruvians' dark eyes and black hair. One study of advertising found that darker-skinned people appeared only rarely in commercials and when they did it was almost exclusively in government-paid spots.

It is not hard to find expressions of the deep divide between people of European descent and the rest. The hugely popular soap opera *Los de arriba y los de abajo*, a sort of Peruvian *Upstairs, Downstairs*, dealt with most of the stereotypes, the usually darker-skinned characters from the working-class area only appearing at the rich family's mansion as gardeners and maids. In spite of a new anti-discrimination law, advertisements until recently were seeking *morenos* (blacks) to work as doormen at the five-star hotels or as bodyguards. A mother out shopping with a uniformed maid carrying the baby is an everyday sight. Poverty and the dearth of jobs mean that many young girls and sometimes boys from poorer families or the provinces work in middle- or upper-class homes. Often these jobs are the only way that youths can finish schooling. The proliferation of maids reinforces an already strong sense of class, that this is a country of masters and servants.

Peru retains a certain colonial snobbery, depicted so tellingly in Alfredo Bryce Echenique's portrait of the careless "beautiful people" of Lima, who share a circuit of private clubs, schools, and even beach resorts. These exclusive centers still exist both in the capital and beyond. In provincial capitals, the "venerable" families hang on to what they see as their separateness, even if their *haciendas* or fortunes are long gone. At some beach resorts near Lima, security guards bar the entrance to the sand, purportedly to keep out non-residents or those bringing food. In practice, this filters out the poorer, darker beach-goers from the more exclusive beaches, making nonsense of the fact that the beaches are supposed to belong to everyone.

Yet many aspects of the old colonial framework have gone with the departure of thousands of foreigners from Peru between the late 1960s to the early 1990s. In a country where drug-trafficking has also left its mark, exclusivity, whether it means private beaches, social clubs, or a residence in a private estate, requires money but not necessarily a name. While Europe was once the benchmark, the model for Peruvians now is Miami, where rich teenagers go to do their shopping.

The election of Alberto Fujimori, the son of Japanese immigrants, has also set new rules in politics. Fujimori's victory had distinct racial overtones. On one level, mixed-race voters rejected the white, rich, intellectual Mario Vargas Llosa, in favor of someone they considered an outsider like them, the candidate they dubbed *El Chino*. Fujimori has since put many people into public posts from both the Japanese and Chinese communities, which have roots in Peru going back at least a century. Yet although he claims to have displaced the *blanquitos* (whites), Fujimori still retains a significant number in his cabinet, where European faces and names dominate.

Fujimori has also shut doors. He has ensured that power is more centralized in Lima than ever, a side-effect of his political strategy to allow no presidential rivals, which has clipped the wings of municipal governments and stopped any independent political movement building strength in the provinces where the traditional parties have lost ground. While no authoritative local leaders emerge, the provinces keep looking to Lima for everything: funds, political ideas, and leaders.

Andean Quechua People

Like the mountains from where they come, the Quechua-speaking people form the backbone of Peru. Those who consider Quechua their mother tongue make up around a fifth of the population, but there are many more descendants of Quechua people who now speak only Spanish. Quechua originally had no alphabet, but the European priests who arrived from the time of the Spanish rule wrote it down. A people used to preserving their history orally, the Quechua have thousands of songs, stories, and dances. Although countless memories have been lost, the remoteness of these communities, isolated until recently by emergency measures, has helped keep alive many traditions, beliefs, dances, and songs.

As people who work the land, Quechua farmers retain a strong sense of respect and intimacy with the earth — which they call the Pachamama —

Festival at Ayaviri

Melchor Lima/TAFOS

the mountains, the forces of nature, the sun, and the stars. Many are zealous Catholics, taking part in religious feasts, but retain other beliefs in parallel. You can still find offerings of coca leaves, corn, and other foods on outdoor stone altars. In the countryside, despite the upheaval of land reform and brutal political violence in the 1980s and 1990s, many villages hang on to traditional agricultural methods, achieving little more than self-sufficiency. Throughout the highlands and particularly in the area around Ayacucho, the unfettered violence of the Shining Path years destroyed an entire lifestyle. Thousands of people migrated either to provincial cities or to Lima, leaving ghost villages in the highest slopes which are only gradually coming back to life.

Throughout the centuries, the Andean Quechua have frequently moved to seek work in the mines and coastal or jungle plantations. Most keep contacts with their home towns. Similarly, in Lima there are now shanty towns set up by people from specific villages who try to keep up traditions by teaching children their customs. But the language fades fast in a capital that makes little allowances for anyone who does not speak Spanish. Since the late 1960s, Quechua has been recognized as an official language along-side Spanish. Yet there is little effort made nationally to promote Quechua or any of the other native tongues, and only the remoteness of many of its speakers helps preserve it in rural areas. In Lima, however, it is given short shrift and there are no television shows in Quechua, nor programs on the main radio stations, and only the most occasional article in the

Schoolchildren, Piura   Susana Pastor/TAFOS

capital's newspapers. For non-Spanish speaking schoolchildren, the official emphasis on Spanish means that many fall behind in schooling.

Black Peruvians

Black slaves were brought to Peru from the sixteenth century, first as domestic servants to the new Spanish ruling class, then as laborers on sugar and cotton plantations. The descendants of these slaves, Peru's black community, are estimated at between two and five per cent of the population and are located almost exclusively on the coast. There are many people born of marriages between blacks and Indians, but the two communities have not shaken off an old and mutual distrust. Since the first black people to come to Peru were often Spanish-speaking house servants, indigenous Peruvians distinguished little between them and their white masters.

During early colonial years, the black immigrants were prominent, coming to represent more than half of Lima's population in the late seventeenth century. Slavery was abolished in Peru in 1854, but with no capital blacks usually had little option but to continue as poorly paid rural farm-hands. There are black communities still dotted up and down the coast, including the heart of the black community, the districts around Chincha, about three hours south of Lima, as well as La Victoria, a working-class neighborhood in the capital itself.

Although black people have achieved scant recognition, they have had a huge influence on what is now considered Peruvian culture. The music of the coast, *criollo* music, is usually played with a *cajón*, a stringed box with one open side which a musician puts between his knees and plays with his bare hands. Afro-Peruvian music and dancing are popular beyond the black communities themselves, while *criollo* dishes such as *anticuchos* (beef heart kebabs), *cau cau* (tripe casserole), and *mazamorra* dessert are black cuisine at its best. Black people have gained prominence in the arts, in cooking, and in sport (Alianza Lima, one of the country's top soccer teams has almost exclusively black players), but none of the 120 members of Congress is Afro-Peruvian. Curiously, in the sierra, where there are few blacks, there is an old tradition that black people bring luck, and Afro-

Peruvians who have lived there say people would surreptitiously touch them or ask them to carry sick infants in the belief that this would bring good luck.

Criollos *and Mestizos*

Originally used to describe the Peruvian-born children of Spaniards, the word *criollo* now identifies many people who live on the coast, regardless of their exact color. Mestizo is the word generally used to describe a Peruvian who is descended from mixed communities, yet the mestizo would still define himself either as a coastal or sierra dweller, and on the coast he might well say he was a *criollo*. More than a community identity, this is a stereotype that mixes up some of the best and worst of coastal culture. A person who is *muy criollo* in Peru, in what can be taken as a compliment or a veiled insult, is very quick on the uptake, taking advantage of any situation with cunning even if it means bending a few rules. The most *criollo* of presidents in recent times was Alan García, himself a mestizo, who seemed able to talk himself out of many compromising situations.

Europeans

Peruvians call most white foreigners *gringos*, and they often refer to Peruvians of European or American descent by the same term, even if Peruvian gringos might have families who have been in the country for centuries. From the arrival of the first Spaniards in the sixteenth century, there has been a constant stream of newcomers, from France, Italy, and Germany, although in nothing like the quantities that arrived in Argentina. There are a very few communities, notably Pozuzo in the *ceja de selva*, where the Austrian-German community has retained some of its native identity.

The majority of Peru's leaders have come from the small and exclusive class of *blanquitos,* and there is a close-knit community of the most prominent families who attend the same English, German, or American schools, have beach houses at the same resorts, and go to the same universities. Peru's wealth is still disproportionately concentrated in this community.

Asian Peruvians

There are two main Asian communities in Peru, the Japanese and the Chinese, both of which have roots going back a century or more. There is undoubtedly a physical similarity between Andeans and Asians, starting with eyes, skin, and dark, straight hair. This outward similarity must have helped the integration of the newcomers into Peruvian society.

Faced with a shortage of rural labor in the mid-nineteenth century, employers turned to China, and it is estimated that between 80,000 and 100,000 "coolies" were brought from that famine-struck country under contracts which offered near-servitude. Since Chinese immigration to Peru began in 1849, some 200,000 immigrants have arrived to date. Many Chinese worked the guano reserves in ghastly conditions, and large numbers died in the process of building the railroads which climbed up the central Andes.

Lima has its own Chinatown near the central market and hundreds of Chinese restaurants known as *chifas* all over the capital. Cooking has been one important Chinese influence on Peru, and a seemingly traditional Peruvian dish like *lomo saltado* is really a stir-fry by another name. If the Chinese community's roots were in virtual slavery in Peru, some descendants of this group have traveled far. One of the most notable success stories is that of the Wong brothers, who developed their father's corner store into the largest and most profitable of Peru's supermarket chains. The Wongs are continuing to extend their interests into banking and real estate.

In the late nineteenth century, a population boom in Japan led to a program to promote migration, and in 1899 Peru received 787 Japanese migrants, supplied by the companies which organized the evacuation of Japanese workers. This started a stream of more than 25,000 migrants by 1929, most of whom were brought to work in the *haciendas* of the coast. At first they received better treatment than the Chinese, but many became disgruntled with deteriorating pay and left for Lima. Japan, meanwhile, actively favored the establishment of a migrant community which could help to secure a supply of important raw materials such as cotton, but this foreign government interest and the fact that the immigrants kept their nationality were to prove a bone of contention. A proliferation of Japanese stores and barber shops, together with the controversy surrounding cotton sales, stirred latent anti-Japanese feeling which erupted from 1930 onwards against a community seen as more introverted and reluctant to intermarry than the Chinese. This hostility came to a head during the Second World War when rumors that the Japanese community was hoarding arms led to open persecution of Japanese businesses, including that of Fujimori's father, and the deportation of more than 1,800 people accused of spying for the enemy to internment camps in the U.S.

This experience left its mark on the Japanese community, now estimated at more than 100,000 people, making it even more reclusive. The hard-working image of this group helped propel Fujimori to electoral victory in 1990, even though the new president did not emerge from the most

An Aguaruna village, Marañon river
Ghislain Pascal/Survival

select ranks of the community, with its private schools and organizations. Under Fujimori, the community gained an unprecedented, and somewhat unwanted, prominence, as many Japanese-descended professionals were appointed to middle-ranking government posts. His election, making him the first leader outside Japan of Japanese extraction, focused Tokyo's interest on Peru, and while much hoped-for private investment failed to arrive, between 1991 and 1996, the Japanese government loaned Peru around $1.6 billion.

Indians of the Selva

The jungle that covers nearly two-thirds of Peru still holds many secrets, not least of which is the real extent of its native people. While anthropologists are divided over whether there are truly uncontacted tribes in the selva, its seems clear that there are still some people living there, surviving from hunting, fishing, and gathering wild fruits, who are fleeing deeper and deeper into the rainforest to evade contact with encroaching woodcutters, gold prospectors, oil workers, and missionaries.

There are several dozen distinct native Indian groups (the census counts 65 groups) living in the selva. While some have been contacted for years, live side by side with mainstream culture, and adopt modern dress, others have been seen only fleetingly and remain elusive. The groups vary in size from a few families to several thousand, such as the Ashaninka, who mostly live in the area near the Rio Ene in central Peru. The Ashaninka, who traditionally wear the *kushma,* a tunic dyed with tree bark, rely on their staple food, yucca, a white turnip-like root vegetable which grows wild, but is also cultivated. From this they make *masato,* a fermented pink-purple alcoholic drink, drunk by everyone from a few months of age. Houses are made of bamboo, with roofs of leaves. They sleep on a raised bamboo or wooden floor inside the huts, which often have no walls. Hunters use bows and arrows, while in the evening others go to the river to fish. Food is cooked over a whole tree trunk which burns for days. There is little difference in their lifestyle, apart from the arrival of schools, from that of hunter-gatherers centuries ago. Health is a great problem, with most of the children malnourished because of the restricted diet, while they lack medicines to cure the malaria spread by infected mosquitoes.

The Ashaninka have suffered one of the most dramatic fates among Peru's indigenous peoples. When Shining Path began operating in their native lands, the rebels took many of them captive as slave-servants or trained them as fighters, while the rest of the tribes were forced to abandon their homelands and flee deep into the jungle. During the emergency years, the area became a no-go zone. Only in the early 1990s did the plight of the refugee communities of the Ashaninka become public. Those who had fled and regrouped in places of refuge were dying of starvation since hunting and fishing had been disrupted; many of the children were yellow with malnutrition and disease. The Ashaninka are now organized in self-defense *rondas* to protect themselves against the rebels and are returning or preparing to return to their villages.

Indian communities face several other threats to their traditional lifestyles and land. The jungle has always been considered a source of riches by Peru's rulers, and the latest arrivals seeking to extract resources from there are the wood companies, gold miners, and multinational oil firms. Although Peru has a law which protects the land rights of indigenous people, its lack of implementation in practice means that some communities have seen their land taken over by outsiders, known as *colonos*, who raze the forest and establish small farms. Forestry companies have cut down trees in large tracts of the high jungle, and there appears to be little effective control of this activity, which is advancing inexorably across the rainforest, reducing hunting lands. Reforestation is legally obligatory, but seldom in evidence in practice.

If the government considers, theoretically at least, that the Indians have the right to live on their lands, it also claims its own monopoly on the sub-soil resources beneath these lands and is granting prospecting rights across the selva. The oil companies have generally reached compensation agreements with indigenous communities whose land they use, but there is widespread fear of contamination once production gets underway on a large scale. Previous oil exploration in Peru has contaminated rivers like the Rio Tigre. Indian groups have also been speaking out for the few non-contacted peoples believed to exist. These isolated people, who have had almost no contact with other peoples, are at risk from diseases against which they have no immunity if they come into contact with any of the outsiders who are entering the jungle in increasing numbers.

Peruvians

There is no doubt that Peru's people are as remarkable as the country's fractured geography and its epic past. The precariousness of daily living for many is matched by a ready wit, limitless ingenuity, and determination of a kind that runs through the many women's organizations set up to confront a chain of crises. Even when economic reality presents seemingly insurmountable problems, people think of ways to get by. Many parents work two shifts, making their working day around sixteen hours long. Teachers often work in at least two schools, on morning and evening shifts. Faced with lack of jobs, others invent a workplace or profession, however unusual. In provincial towns, you can hire women to cry at funerals. In all cemeteries, particularly on the Day of the Dead, young boys offer to clean up graves or bring water for flowers, while psalm-singers are for hire to hold lay services or chant psalms before any grave.

Everywhere people are engaged in a battle not just to get by, but to get better too. Many study at night school or mix a full-time job with university courses, sometimes piecing degrees together over many years. Foreign language institutes of all prices can be found in Lima, with English the most sought-after.

Bureaucracy and coima

One of Peru's most enduring inheritances from Spain is its labyrinthine bureaucracy. In most ministries, there is at least one person whose job is to stamp the piles of documents which arrive and leave daily. The government has made efforts to simplify some processes, but in general Peruvians cling to the need for legal documents and vast lists of certificates. For every unbelievably time-consuming process there are several fast-track options. One are the *tramitadores*, who spring up wherever there are long lines, know people on the inside of the bank or government office, and offer to undertake all the bureaucratic steps — for a small fee. Others sell their place in particularly lengthy lines.

The antithesis of the bureaucratic nightmare is the *coima*, a usually small bribe which speeds up your documents' passage through the system, gives a judge a slightly better opinion of your case, or induces temporary amnesia in police officers who had been apparently outraged at your driving the wrong way up a one-way street. Only a few years ago, *coimas* were an integral part of many bureaucratic processes, and without these informal payments papers languished unattended. Again, a change in attitude, particularly in the state sector, means this is no longer true of all offices, but there is no doubt that *coimas* can still be found in a country where the use of *vara* (influence) and *compadrazgo* (jobs for the boys) have been common practice for decades.

The most persistent *coimeros* or bribe-takers are the low-paid police, who still consider these small contributions a perk of the job. Around Christmas, police seeking bribes as low as 1 sol ($0.50) a time sometimes put up inexplicable road-

PERU

Peru's indigenous peoples make up the majority of the population. Despite centuries of discrimination, their traditions remain intact in dress, music and festivals.

Women from Pisac
Tony Morrison/South American Pictures

The floating Los Uros islands on Lake Titicaca
Julio Etchart/Reportage

Harvesting barley on Inca terraced fields
(Tony Morrison/south American Pictures)

THE FESTIVAL - DRINKING, DANCING, MUSIC AND DISPLAY

Weaving, Taquile island
(Julio Etchart/Reportage)

Drinking
(Annie Bungeroth)

Spinning, Chinchero
(Tony Morrison/South American Pictures)

The mestizo hat. One for everyday wear and one for special occasions. the hats are re-whitened from time to time.
(Annie Bungeroth)

Music
(Annie Bungeroth)

Dancing
(Tony Morrison/South American Pictures)

Inti Raymi, festival to worship the sun
(Tony Morrison/South American Pictures)

PEOPLE OF THE AMAZON

Ashaninka children
(Ana Cecilia/Survival)

An Ashaninka woman preparies yucca
(Ana Cecilia/Survival-)

Shipibo woman sewing
(Ana Cecilia/Survival)

blocks outside shanty towns or stop motorists and "persuade" them to buy tickets for raffles which, almost inevitably, never take place. The courts were traditionally considered to run on *coimas*, although depending on the case the cost of "buying a judge" can be much higher. A campaign to clean up the judiciary has weeded out a handful of judges caught receiving small bribes of $100 or $200 a time. However, it appears that bigger fish remain.

Society

Whatever aspect of social provision is considered in Peru, there is one common denominator: there is not enough to go round. Although officials welcome the fact that the total number of poor fell from 55 per cent in 1991 to 45.3 per cent in 1995, society is a litany of unfulfilled needs. Peru is not the worst off of the South American countries, but its adverse geography, guerrilla war, and steep drop in income in the 1980s mean it is among those countries with the most ground to recover.

The private research group Cuanto estimated the number of poor in 1996 at 49 per cent of the population, up from the 1994 figure, while it claimed that those in extreme poverty, unable to meet their basic requirements for food, total around 16.6 per cent, or nearly four million people. The state figures for extreme poverty are even higher, at 19.3 per cent. The reality behind the figures is grim: 34 per cent of children with chronic malnutrition, 38 per cent of homes without running water, 36 per cent without electricity, 30 per cent with no access to public health services, 50 infant deaths for every 1,000 births.

Population

People in the countryside talk of seeing medical field tents set up in rural towns with the cheerful-sounding announcement of a "festival of tube-tying." An aggressive campaign of family planning, including sterilization, intensified under Fujimori, has helped slow an already declining birth rate, down from more than three per cent annually at its peak to less than two per cent. The government ran head-on into conflict with the Catholic church over the promotion of artificial planning methods and allegations that unsuspecting mothers were being sterilized without really understanding what was going on. Abortion is illegal in Peru, but anyone who needs to can find out where to have a pregnancy terminated. This de facto freedom means there is no strong grassroots battle to legalize abortion. Those with cash can find a private doctor, while there are many less secure methods practiced among poorer women which on occasion end in death or serious infection. Non-governmental organizations estimate that there are around 270,000 illegal abortions a year in Peru.

Health

Only two-thirds of Peruvians have access to public health services. In rural areas, many people have no service except that of the local *curanderos*, self-taught healers who use herbs and other means to treat patients. Not only is there a high rate of infant mortality, four times that of neighboring Chile and Colombia, but the figures become far steeper in some rural areas where more than one in ten infants die within a year of birth. Equally worrying is that so many women die each year in childbirth or from botched abortions, figures which medical experts blame on lack of education about basic health risks and a still limited spread of primary health care.

Yet there have been some improvements in health care which are beginning to show. Since 1985, the Health Ministry has more than halved the number of infant deaths from illness related to diarrhea. Times have changed from the days when child vaccination campaigns in the country led the police to cordon off the exits of the local market and almost force mothers to have their babies immunized. Now there is far greater information on vaccinations, and 96 per cent of infants have been immunized against tuberculosis and 95 per cent against diphtheria, compared to 48 per cent and 14 per cent in 1980 respectively.

Although health services are nominally free for those inscribed in the social security system, even in the capital families usually have to find the money to pay for medicines prescribed in hospital. Medicines are expensive and it is common for adults to buy tablets singly. Since they rarely finish a course of medicine, they are often face the risk that the illness they are treating will return strengthened and become chronic. In areas of greatest need, poverty and malnutrition remain the root of many illnesses, while malnourished children suffer severe developmental problems which translate into continuing health concerns throughout life.

Education

Peru had a university before the USA. San Marcos University, founded in 1551, was the first such institution in South America, and despite all difficulties still continues teaching. Yet notwithstanding its long record in education, Peru is woefully short of resources. There are around eleven million school-age children in Peru, most of them at state schools. Although provision of schooling has extended greatly in the last 30 years, concerns remain over the quality of what is taught as well as perennial shortages. State teachers have seen their salaries slide and many have left education to seek a living in more commercial pursuits. Poorer schoolchildren find it hard to buy pencils and notebooks and there are few textbooks in most state schools. Around one million school-age children, meanwhile, do not

Working children, mining at Madre de Dios   Susana Pastor/TAFOS

go to classes at all, but work, and of every 100 who start primary school a quarter abandon schooling. In rural areas, lack of interest is put down in part to the fact that schooling is usually in Spanish, and those whose native language is Quechua, Aymara, or one of the languages spoken in the jungle find it harder to keep up, often abandoning classes to help their families on the land. The underfunded state system is perhaps only held together by the commitment of often young rural teachers who go and live in the remotest villages, from where they sometimes have to journey for days to pick up their monthly wage of 420 soles ($158.00) per month.

The impoverished situation of rural state schools is offset up by the harshly competitive business of private schooling in the capital, where better-off parents struggle to pay a few thousand dollars just to enroll a child into one of the smarter schools, even before the monthly fees and long list of supplies. Aside from the few state universities, private institutions are proliferating, even if there seems little relationship between the number of places open for professionals such as lawyers or engineers and openings available in the job market. State universities, plagued by strikes since the 1970s, were until recently the butt of jokes because students were taking eight, ten, or even more years to obtain a first degree. Reorganization and the decline in influence of radical political groups, most especially Shining Path, among both student and professor ranks have returned these to normality, although most tutors have to supplement teaching at a state university with another private-sector job.

Crime

The roads into richer residential estates in Lima are barred by gates and armed security guards. Tiny wooden kiosks to house the youths who will watch over the block day and night, known universally as *guachimanes* (watchmen), are sprouting in middle-class areas. One of the few sectors where job prospects are looking up is in security. A spate of kidnappings *al paso*, where thieves pick up their victims virtually at random, is petrifying richer Limeños, as common crime replaces rebel violence as one of people's main fears. Petty crime is nothing new, but there are worries that crime is becoming more organized, better armed, and more widespread. Throughout the country, a police force which is underpaid and discredited for its openness to quick bribes is unable to stem the rising tide of crime. Even so, Lima remains far safer than more heavily-armed capitals like Bogota or Caracas. One answer in the better organized shanty towns has been the creation of neighborhood security groups, such as in Villa El Salvador. These forces, styled on the peasant self-defense *rondas* of the countryside, are likely to spread. In more wealthy areas, the vans and cars of the Serenazgo municipal security force drive around constantly in a bid to keep the peace. Yet in other parts of Peru a frontier-style lawlessness still reigns, from the most outlying shanty towns, where every so often a thief turns up beaten and crucified at dawn after being lynched, to the jungle gold rush or drug towns where more dangerous criminals are still too great a match for the police. The spread of gang violence by the so-called *barras bravas* or soccer gangs is a new concern in Lima, running side by side with high youth unemployment and poverty.

Church

Of all the social organizations in Peru, the Catholic Church is probably the most influential and complex. Invasions to build new squatter townships always leave a space for a yet-to-be-built church building, and many nuns and priests are working out their vocation living in the desert settlements with the poor. Peruvian priest Gustavo Gutiérrez was one of the most prominent proponents of the liberation theology which swept through the Catholic Church in Latin America from the late 1960s onwards. In areas like Puno in the south, the radical clergy supported land protests and helped peasants in their fight for greater rights, which in turn was crucial in preventing Shining Path from making deep inroads into that area. There is a sharp divide, however, between the clergy in Peru, who see it as their priority to be on the side of the poor, and the conservative hierarchy which often appears to be in place just to rein in the more successful popular programs of its radical priests. Peru still depends heavily on foreign clergy to staff its churches, and there is a serious shortage of local vocations to the priesthood. A lack of priests has left churches in many rural villages unattended.

The church suffered a serious dent in its authority during the clash with President Alberto Fujimori over family planning. Fujimori appeared to win the battle, with most agreeing with the need for a slowdown in population growth. Yet the greatest threat to the church's traditional influence has been the spreading of evangelical Protestant groups in Peru. In many rural villages, while the Catholic church is left padlocked, the Jehovah's Witnesses or Mormons, Adventists, or another Protestant group has set up a prayer group and a meeting house. Often backed by cash from the United States, these churches have established themselves throughout Lima and in other urban centers, offering varied attractions of strict discipline, soccer fields and English classes. There are now estimated to be around 1.5 million members of evangelical churches in Peru and their mounting influence was proven when they supported Fujimori in his 1990 election campaign, ensuring a strong performance in the first round through door-to-door lobbying.

Other Social Organizations

Offices of many non-government organizations in Peru still bear the signs of their most uncertain decade. Visitors often find the entrance protected by bars and a series of heavy locks, a relic of the years when Shining Path turned its fury on anyone who dared to help others from outside its own sectarian ranks.

Political violence devastated Peruvian grassroots and social organizations which faced Shining Path threats on the one hand, and intimidation from security forces who suspected these same groups of supporting the rebels on the other. Many union leaders, mayors, and community activists were killed by Shining Path. Society has yet to recover from this blow. Grassroots organizations working in shanty towns or within the women's movement managed to ride out the worst years and even helped to turn the tide of popular feeling against Shining Path. Yet these groups seem scared to move outside their orbit of addressing immediate and practical needs into dealing with wider political problems. Although Peruvians are greatly disillusioned with organized parties of all shades, the rebel insurgency wrought its greatest damage among other left-wing groups which simply did not know how to combat it.

An efficient intelligence service, originally expanded to fight the rebel threat, has become more powerful, acting as a deterrent for anyone who speaks out too loudly and dissuading people from joining groups considered to oppose the government. Organizations concerned with consumer action, human rights, ethnic identity, and women's issues exist in Peru, but are

The festival of Our Lord of Q'Oylloritti   *Annie Bungeroth*

very small. Bodies like Foro Democrático, which works with focus groups
concerned with fomenting a democratic culture in the country, say that an
absence of institutions and a weakened civil society are the main obstacles
to establishing a real democracy in Peru. One of the few groups to fill the
political vacuum, in rural communities at least, are the self-defense groups,
the *ronderos*. Many community leaders and village chiefs have emerged
through these organizations, which enjoy a high level of respect and popular
participation.

5   CULTURE: ART AND IDENTITY

Don't expect to find Peruvian culture in grand opera houses or labyrinthine art galleries. Culture is elsewhere; it is all around you. Probably the only exhibitions of "high culture" are those which dig deep into the past, in the luxurious artistry of the Moche, in the display of the glorious gold jewelry and weapons found in the tombs of the Lords of Sipán. Modern culture is more diffuse, still rooted in region and race, and, for most Peruvians, culture is part of daily life. Art and music express the distinct identities of different regions, varying from the extravagant dance troupes of La Candelaria festival in Puno to the swirl of the *marinera* dancers in Trujillo, a continuous link between a gregarious people and their need to express themselves.

Although some renowned artists, like Fernando de Szyszlo, have rightly found a place on international collectors' walls, on a different plane, many other, often anonymous, artists are struggling to take regional crafts like pottery and weaving a step higher up the aesthetic scale to art. Some like Eddie Sulca with tapestries and Edilberto Jiménez with *retablos,* tiny sculpted figures portraying typical scenes set inside small painted wooden houses, are on their way to succeeding. But culture still belongs to the masses when threadbare villagers from distant hillsides come together in their thousands amid exploding fireworks towers and colossal waxen biers in processions which are a pageant of emotion and theater as moving as any modern drama.

Music and Dance

For Peruvians music is not so much a spectacle as something which invites participation. Parties often turn into sing-song renditions of favorite *valses*, while a guest will pull out a drawer from any nearby chest, empty it, and use it as a makeshift *cajón,* the stringed wooden box which is the heartbeat of *criollo* music. Family parties which begin with an unfriendly-looking circle of chairs lined around a room disintegrate into chaos once the dancing begins. Dancing takes a thousand forms, and depending on where people come from, it can be the almost ceremonial stepping of the *huayno*, the energetic stamping of the *huaylas,* interspersed on the coast by the light-hearted waltzing of *criollo* music, the elegant coquetry of the *marinera,* the imported snappy twirls of salsa and the sexy fluidity and pounding rhythm of the *negroide.* And that is without mentioning rock and pop.

There are hundreds of musicians, singers, and groups in Peru worth hearing. The late Chabuca Granda, a singer and songwriter, embodied the *jarana*, the *criollo* musical nightlife of *valses* and guitars. Her most famous song, *La Flor de la canela*, has become an unofficial hymn to Lima and a bygone golden age of bohemian nights. Eva Ayllón, is one of the best loved women singers of *criollo* music, while another Afro-Peruvian woman, Susana Baca, has recently recorded with Talking Heads' David Byrne.

For a famous male *criollo* voice try the feisty Oscar Avilés, especially when he shares a stage with Afro-Peruvian Arturo "Zambo" Cavero's throaty songs and rhythm. There are guitarists of all kinds, a legacy of the first Spaniards, with piquant *criollo* and black music masterfully played by Felix Casaverde, or *huaynos* and *yaravis*, a kind of Andean lament, rendered classical in the hands of Raúl García Zarate, or given a gypsy soul by guitarist and songwriter Manuelcha Prado. There is a huge market in folk music which treads a line between the formal and informal economies: you can sample hundreds of different local styles on cassettes in the maze of stalls in Mesa Redonda, behind Lima's chaotic central market.

Regional folk has not stood still, however. The relevance of traditional music was clear in the early 1980s, when new protest songs in *huayno* style emerged from Ayacucho, the city at the heart of the Shining Path violence. Among the new songwriters was teacher Ranulfo Fuentes, who captured a spirit of defiance and anguish. In the tense atmosphere of the time, some of these songs were considered incendiary and it was risky to sing them. Fuentes' song *El Hombre* begins: *"Yo no quiero ser el hombre, que se ahoga en su llanto, de rodillas hechas llagas que se postra al tirano."* ("I do not want to be the man, who drowns in his tears, with his knees torn from prostrating himself before the tyrant.")

Yet the distinct tastes of regions and ethnic groups have started to blur with the flood of migration to the cities, mainly to Lima. The music of the *pueblos jóvenes* is *chicha*, originally the name of a fruit- or corn-based fermented drink. A kind of speeded-up *huayno*, *chicha* blares on the tiny buses which race each other for passengers through the snarled-up Lima traffic, or in the popular *chichodromos*, where hundreds of workers go on their Sundays off. *Chicha* is a meeting of Peru's highlands with the warm, tropical coast, not just of Peru, but of Colombia and other Latin countries. Like salsa, it is grouped as *música tropical,* and although so far it has been widely adopted as a favorite dance music by Peru's urban working class, it is now breaking into new markets like Argentina and Bolivia.

Media and Politics

Around every newspaper kiosk you can see a cluster of people lingering, reading the front page headlines of the dailies which are hung out with clothes pegs. That is about the nearest most people get to reading a newspaper or magazine, a luxury for all but a tiny group. The "yellow press,"

Newspapers in the small Andean town of Chachapoyas

Tony Morrison/South American Pictures

sensationalist papers written in raunchy slang, is gaining readership. The combined sales of those with names like *Aja, El Mañanero,* and *El Chino*, distinguished particularly by the excessive appearance of women's almost bare behinds, is now overtaking the sales of the staid broadsheet *El Comercio*, whose top selling point is its near monopoly grasp on the classified ads market. The sensationalist press was the launch-pad for the election campaign of showgirl Susy Díaz, who succeeded in winning a seat in Congress in 1995. She won attention for posing with the number of her candidacy painted in lipstick on her near-nude bottom.

There are few influential provincial newspapers. Radio is far more important in getting news to Peruvians, particularly since limited plane routes mean that it would be hard to get newspapers to much of the country on the same day. The all-pervasive Radioprogramas del Perú, which has round-the-clock rolling news and chat shows dominates the market, although in Lima, newcomer Cadena Peruana de Noticias now follows a similar formula. There are countless local radio stations which cover far-flung areas, making radio the country's most ubiquitous medium. The independent news magazine *Caretas* is the most widely read among the chattering classes. Firmly in opposition during the Fujimori years, it has survived economic hardship and dwindling advertising revenue to continue to give a pointed, usually thoughtful version of the news, explaining a lot of the behind-the-scenes gossip which is the stuff of Peruvian politics.

Television, however, is the most influential medium in mass terms. It also reaches into huge tracts of the country and, as the comic strip in *La República* implies, the *calatos*, the poor who have no clothes, jobs, and barely have homes, nonetheless have a television. Apart from the wide selection of soap-operas from Mexico, Venezuela, and Brazil and, more recently, Peruvian-made series, the most important shows are three investigative news programs shown on Sunday which often tread a fine line between political manipulation and sensational scoops. With a fierce battle for limited advertising revenue among the six main private channels (one channel is now funded by an Evangelical group and another is state-funded), television still offers an overdose of imported U.S. series, quiz shows whose constant references to sponsors make them seem like extended commercials, and raunchy Benny Hill-style comedy shows.

Film production in Peru is now rare. The boost given to film production by President García, who made it obligatory for cinemas to show Peruvian-made shorts before the main films, was swept away with the neo-liberal model. Some Peruvian filmmakers and directors have received recognition abroad, like Luis Llosa and Francisco Lombardi, whose *La Boca del lobo*, a haunting account of an army massacre in a remote Andean village, is unique in capturing the taut emotion of the dirty war years and achieving popular acclaim.

Literature

Peru's most famous living author, Mario Vargas Llosa, like many of the country's best-known writers, has lived much of his life outside Peru, yet he returns to the country again and again for inspiration. Vargas Llosa is probably unmatched among Peru's novelists in his search for the perfect technique to reflect what he considers a hypocritical and often disintegrating society. His earlier novels like *The Time of the Hero*, a tale of lost schoolboy innocence, and *Aunt Julia and the Scriptwriter*, a joyful, semi-auto-biographical account of a love affair between the writer and his aunt, are more accessible. Yet the tautly controlled *Conversation in the Cathedral*, where Vargas Llosa teases and puzzles the reader by running together phrases from conversations and narrative which happened years apart, unwrapping the story like the most complex Japanese origami, is probably his greatest work.

The writer's earliest works are the most rewarding; his later works are more inconsistent and introspective. Vargas Llosa's venture into politics, and especially his unsuccessful bid for the presidency in 1990, was also an episode which estranged the Peruvian public from him. He emerged so crushed from that experience that he subsequently adopted Spanish nationality, a move which most Peruvians found untenable. Yet his lordly manner, cosmopolitan lifestyle, and place at the heart of Lima's white intellectual elite have always made him a distant figure for many Peruvians, even though his prose is widely admired. He received his first honorary doctorate in Peru only in 1997.

lfredo Bryce Echenique, despite cutting a different figure from the patrician Vargas Llosa and giving the impression of being permanently overwhelmed by life, self-effacing and almost lost, really comes from the same place. Beside Vargas Llosa, Bryce is Peru's best-known living novelist. Like him, Bryce has lived abroad for most of his life, teaching at the Sorbonne in Paris and writing in different parts of Spain. His background is that of the wealthy circle of Lima's beautiful people, portrayed with an irony tinged with sadness in his best work, *A World for Julius*. The boy, Julius, relates with puzzled innocence the goings-on in his life among a very polite, yet ultimately heartless set, where he obviously feels completely unloved and lost. Bryce's greatest touch is his irony, but his popularity is more limited than that of Vargas Llosa to Peruvians who can appreciate his telling swift portraits.

Despite living in Paris for most of his life, poet César Vallejo (1892-1938) has been adopted as the model of many contemporary intellectuals, and his poems still stun with their brilliance and transmission of deep dislocation and suffering. One of the best known is *Los heraldos negros* (The Black Heralds), which opens with an outpouring of sorrow and confusion: *"Hay golpes en la vida, tan fuertes ... Yo no sé! / Golpes como el odio de Dios; como si ante ellos, / la resaca de todo lo sufrido / se empozara en el alma .. Yo no se"* ("There are blows in life that are so hard ... I don't know! / Blows like the wrath of God; as though in the face of them / the dregs of all suffering / were stagnating in the soul ... I don't know.")

While there is little Peruvian literature in Quechua, apart from the vast repertoire of songs, a line of writers from the *indigenista* movement did emerge. They drew their inspiration from the world of the indigenous Andean, in some cases finding in the Indian the personification of inno-cence and good. The best of these writers was José María Arguedas, a *mestizo*, who learned his Quechua among the kitchen servants. Arguedas' novel *Todas las sangres* (All the Bloods), which includes several Quechua songs and words, paints all the sectors of a disintegrating Andean society with the personalities and prejudices of his characters, from the free peas-ant farmer to the great *hacendado*. However idealized his picture of indig-

Roasting meat at the Vindinia wine tasting festival *Annie Bungeroth*

enous culture, Arguedas gives an insight into this society which feels unmistakably authentic. From the same school, Cusco photographer Martín Chambi, with his beautifully lit studies of people of all classes, festivities, and scenery, complements this written record of the richness of Andean society.

Food

Peru is rivaled in Latin America only by Mexico in the variety of its cuisine. Peruvians abroad usually reserve their greatest homesickness for their food. On a Peruvian menu you will find dishes that date back to pre-Inca times, like the biting *cebiche*, fish marinated in lime juice with onion and hot peppers *(ají)*, alongside *criollo* food like *cau cau* (tripe) which has a strong black influence.

Peruvian cooking is generally a time-consuming business, and there seems no limit to the effort people are prepared to put in. One example is the *pachamanca*, a kind of underground barbecue typical of the sierra. Preparations take a day, involving the digging of a huge hole in the ground which is lined with hot porous rocks. Different kinds of meat, beans, potatoes, sweet potatoes, and *humitas* (corn cakes) are put inside, the food is covered over and the hole is filled in. The food cooks for hours under the earth and comes out more tender and delicious than in any exquisite many-starred restaurant. Often the best food experiences are the simple ones: such as the dozens of fresh fruit juices available at the market (to be safe, ask for a mix with orange juice instead of water); or a boiled cob of sweet corn, with huge kernels, bought from a roadside seller in the mountains, eaten hot with fresh goat's cheese; or a glass of *emoliente*, the green, yellow, brown, and orange herbal essences which are served hot from kiosks to warm early bus travelers or students in winter. The uninitiated should beware of the famous pisco sour, the cocktail based on pisco brandy, egg whites and lime juice, which tastes deceptively like home-made lemonade but packs a late punch. The other national drink, apart from the beer which is the staple of most parties, is the bright yellow soft drink, Inca Kola, which runs neck-and-neck with

Football in the sierra   *Mauri Quispecondori/TAFOS*

Coca-Cola in sales. Although it looks garish and is on the sweet side, it can become habit-forming when served ice-cold.

Sport

Soccer is Peru's sporting passion (followed at a distance by women's volleyball), although the national team has developed a reputation for flashy technique but ineffective goal-scoring in recent years. Peru failed to qualify for the 1994 World Cup and the national team's new star is a Brazilian who has adopted Peruvian nationality, a symptom that the sport, while it still inspires passion, is somewhat in the doldrums.

The two classic Lima teams are Alianza, a mostly Afro-Peruvian team whose stadium is in the black, working-class area of Matute, and Universitario (abbreviated to "La U"), its bitter rival. In recent years, Sporting Cristal, backed by brewery giant Backus and Johnson, has had more championship success than the classic teams, but the capital and even the country is still split on U-Alianza lines.

WHERE TO GO, WHAT TO SEE

The first thing a traveler to Peru should check, even before looking at a map, is the calendar. Peru lives a year-round whirl of fiestas which can transform sleepy towns into wild water-throwing parties or centers of ornate holy processions which draw people from miles around. It helps to know about these changes. The fiestas have two roots: the Catholic Church calendar and the agricultural year, with celebrations related to harvest and spring. Mix some all-night revelry at a local fiesta with some off-season solitude which allows you just to look and wonder at the beauty of magical Andean lakes, of a turquoise green only found in fairy tales, or to travel off the beaten track on the back of a truck with the wind in your hair and the mountains rising up on all sides.

Peru has three faces, the coast, the sierra, and the jungle. A visitor who wants to experience all three on a fairly short trip will need to fly, as Peru's fractured geography makes it hard to rush around by road. Check the calendar again to find out when the rainy season hits the Andes (December to March) as this can make road travel difficult and trekking, such as on the Inca Trail linking Cusco with Machu Picchu, a washout.

Two of the key festival dates along the spine of the Andes are Carnival, the weekend before Ash Wednesday, and Semana Santa (Holy Week), which ends on Easter Sunday. Recently christened as the Carnival capital of Peru, Cajamarca, in the northern sierra, hosts a messy, raucous carnival week with many processions and dances but where the fun revolves around slapstick water-and-paint throwing which leaves you constantly drenched. Don't wear your best clothes, get into the spirit, regress to childhood, and have fun. Carnival is celebrated in most of the Andes and there is always some element of water-fights, even on all Sundays in February in Lima. At a typical carnival you can see villagers from the *puna* with simple *quenas* and tiny hand drums, hundred-strong groups with bands, and the comical *comparsas* (dance troupes) led by men in drag and figures making fun of local authorities. If you miss carnival in the towns, outlying villages often continue the celebration with traditional *cortamontes*, where a tree is decorated with gifts and dancers in pairs take turns at trying to cut it down. Be careful, because the person whose blow fells the tree hosts the party the following year.

At the southern point of the Andes, on the border between Lake Titicaca and Bolivia, the fiesta of the Virgen de la Candelaria takes place in the first week of February, unless this coincides with carnival, with stunning

Day of the Dead   *Annie Bungeroth*

dance groups in colorful costumes and processions with traditional music, including virtual orchestras of panpipe players, the famous *sicuris*.

Next on the fiesta calendar is Semana Santa, which is celebrated in most of Peru with processions in which the most revered statues from local churches are paraded around the streets. Among the cities with celebrations are Huaraz, Tarma, the center of flower-growing in the central Andes, and Arequipa in the south. Ayacucho has the most famous Holy Week in Peru, its daily processions inspiring fervent devotion among locals, with flower carpets, firework castles, and the arrival of hundreds of horses and llamas loaded with *chamizo* (gorse) which is burned on Easter Sunday at dawn.

For those in search of a full-scale fiesta, Inti Raymi in Cusco, on June 24, coinciding with the half-year solstice, is one of the biggest. Held in the Sacsayhuamán fortress on the outskirts of the city, it is a great pageant, but there are many tourists. Cusco also has Corpus Cristi, another moveable feast. The coast has its own pleasures, with the Spring festival in Trujillo in September bringing out the dancers of the *marinera*, a swirling, courtly style, while in the black communities of Chincha, south of Lima, you can hear the rhythm of the *cajón* and the more sensual dances of *negroide*. Lima's Señor de los Milagros (on several dates in October) has its roots in the city's black community and is a spectacle of mass devotion, with a heady mix of costumes and incense, but it is for watching, rather than for joining in.

In all Peruvian fiestas, the holy is mixed with the unholy. Almost all of the country's feast days, including the Day of the Dead on November 1, celebrated at the country's cemeteries, involve drinking, eating, and dancing until the revelers, often literally, drop in their tracks. There are too many fiestas to mention them all. There are hundreds of little-known village celebrations which can afford a real taste of rural life.

Many people would advise visitors to skip Lima all together. The capital, particularly when shrouded in the mist that rolls in off the sea for several months a year, has a reputation for being dour, dangerous, or dirty. Yet it is as safe or safer than other South American capitals, and, as home to more than a third of Peruvians, is a key to understanding the country. Migration to the city is "Peruvianizing" Lima, where you can find food, crafts, music, and people from every corner of the country. Particularly in summer, it is worth spending time dawdling round the seaside neighborhood of Barranco, home to the city's bohemians and part of the Lima coastline which is gradually filling up with high-rise apartment blocks. By day, a charming, if down-at-heel square, Barranco center brims at night as people pack into the countless bars and *peñas*. Nearby Miraflores repays a visit and has some of the best restaurants. Although it is more of a commercial center, you can sit outside, drink a capuccino, and watch couples and families in the popular park. Most of the country's arts and crafts can be found at the Indian market in Miraflores.

Years of poverty, neglect, and flight to newer or more prosperous districts have left the historic center of Lima largely in the hands of the poor, street traders, and students. Once an elegant colonial area, the center is run down, with the ornate wooden balconies of some houses serving only to hang out the washing of the residents crammed inside, often a family to a room. The main square, recently remodeled, is kept pristine, with the government palace and the cathedral, and there are several museums and churches worth visiting. Walk round the center, but go with someone who knows the area, as you can easily stray. The barring of most traffic from the historic center and an ongoing attempt to regulate street traders promise to return some order to the once-proud area.

Although Lima is the administrative capital, Cusco is the tourist capital. From the stunning Inca stonework on which the main buildings still stand and the long Inca-designed streets to the charming red-tiled roofs and magnificent churches, Cusco is solid history. The city is a magnet for all kinds of people attracted by the mystical qualities of the Inca heritage and the fraternity of mystics who live there. It is also a gateway to the beautiful

The Inca trail

Kimball Morrison/South American Pictures

Sacred Valley of the Incas, where day tours take in huge Inca forts and villages, but whose scenery on a sunny day is just as awe-inspiring. From Cusco you can set off to do river-rafting, walk the Inca Trail, or travel to the Manú national park. But the most traveled route is to the train station, from where you can go to Machu Picchu, the famous Inca sanctuary, long hidden in the Urubamba valley, high on a mountain peak. To sit on the smooth, giant Inca stones and gaze down at the rich green foliage and the snaking river is to feel as though you are on top of the world.

Perhaps the only downside of Cusco, apart from altitude sickness, is that it is one of the few places in Peru where you are made to feel like a tourist. Even street children tugging at your arm for money ask for "one dollar." Yet generally, with the exception of Cusco, tourism is still fairly sparse in Peru and gringos (American/European tourists) are welcomed or curiously eyed as a relative novelty.

The Andes is for many the real heart of Peru, particularly since it lags behind the coast in modernity. You can pick from the lush, green farmlands and hot springs of Cajamarca, or the snow-covered mountains and clear lakes of Huaraz, where mountain-climbers are tempted by the Alpamayo, feted as the "prettiest" mountain in the world. Another historic site, the pre-Inca Chavín de Huántar, is a reminder of the grandeur of that period. You can get a less pampered view of the Andes in Ayacucho, peaceful now after years of troubles, where 33 churches in the small city testify to its former wealth. Dip down to Huancayo, a prosperous trading city which is now only five hours' drive from Lima in the Mantaro Valley, or to the flower fields of Tarma.

Arequipa, with its elegant atmosphere, is the city least likely to jolt a newcomer. Set against the Misti volcano, the "white city" is home to the

A hummingbird - the Nazca Lines   *Tony Morrison/South American Pictures*

Santa Catalina convent which stirs the imagination to times when a lively community of rich nuns lived behind its walls. From there you can visit the Colca canyon, deeper than the Grand Canyon. Flanked by impressive agricultural terraces and traditional villages, visitors can see beautiful scenery and glimpse majestic condors.

There are beaches of varying qualities along the length of the coast and surfers find some of the world's longest and most challenging waves off Peru. Although Peruvian beaches are not on a par with the white sands of the Caribbean, there are relaxing resorts in the north, where the sun is practically guaranteed all year long. Only a few hours from Lima, you can sail to the Islas Ballestas, which teem with sea lions and seabirds, and on the mainland see signs of early Paracas culture.

Peru is full of mysteries and one puzzle is clearly visible from the air near the coastal town of Nazca. Small planes fly over the Nazca Lines, a series of animal figures and geometric shapes cut into the desert, which some say are a primitive calendar or signs to a flying god. Another Peruvian enigma can be experienced at Huancabamba, near Piura, a village of healers, who use the hallucinatory cactus plant, *ayahuasca*, and ritual bathing in sacred lakes to cure ailments of all sorts. Much of the north coast is famous for magical healing and there are many folk-healers, known as *chamanes*. *Ayahuasca* and other plants which induce hallucinations are also used in the jungle by Indian communities to heal patients, cast out curses, or experience another mental dimension.

In the jungle, you can visit Iquitos, the capital of the Peruvian Amazon, or start further south in Puerto Maldonado or Tarapoto. There are several national parks in the jungle, including Tambopata and Manú. The beauty of reserves like the Manú, where you can drift down rivers seeing red parrots and swinging monkeys amid a vast variety of plant life, offers an unforgettable introduction to one of the world's richest natural resources.

TIPS FOR TRAVELERS

Customs

In Peru, women or men meeting women usually greet with one kiss on the cheek. Men shake hands. When introduced, Peruvians will probably expect to greet visitors in the same way. Time-keeping is erratic. Peruvians think nothing of arriving an hour or so late on social occasions. You may prefer to specify that you want to meet *"en punto"* to make sure it is clear you expect to meet more or less at an exact time.

Safety

As in most tourist destinations in Latin America, theft occurs in Peru. Do not wander around with expensive belongings, and, if possible, go out sightseeing without a bag. Bus and train stations are notorious for petty theft, so take special care and never leave bags unattended on a train. On arrival in a city, consult with hotel staff about the best areas to walk around in. If you expect to travel off the beaten track, remember that there are still areas in Peru that are under emergency rule where you may need to register with local military authorities on arrival. Consult with your embassy if you plan this kind of trip. Be aware that occasionally border officials or police can seek a small bribe.

Health and Hygiene

The main hazard for the newcomer is water, which is generally unsafe to drink. Choose bottled water or water you know has been boiled or sterilized. When traveling outside Lima, toilet facilities can be poor and occasionally grim. Always carry toilet paper with you as this may not be provided. Paper should be discarded in garbage cans as water pressure is often too low to cope. In many areas, water supply is restricted. Ask on arrival at a hotel if this is the case and what hours water is turned on.

Eating

Apart from the most exclusive spots, most restaurants in Peru have a set lunch menu. If you ask for *"el menú"* this is what you will be served. The menu is called *"la carta."* The set menu has its advantages since it is ready and will be served almost immediately and it is usually cheap. Even cafes popular with visitors, like the Cafe de la Paz in Miraflores, have a menu which is tasty and good value for money.

Money

U.S. dollars are a parallel currency in Peru. In Lima, you can pay at most supermarkets, better restaurants, and stores in dollars. If taking dollars in cash to Peru, ask your bank to pick out bills that are not torn or damaged in any way. If bills are ripped you may have trouble changing them, even in a bank, or might get a worse rate of exchange. Changing dollars on the street is extremely common and in some areas like San Isidro and Miraflores the moneychangers wear an ID card. However, the difference between the parallel rate and that paid by banks is probably less than $1 per $100, so newcomers would probably be safer to use banks.

Shopping

When shopping, remember that there are layers of different economies and you might be paying overheads for the privilege of shopping in an attractive shopping center, as opposed to a street market. In markets (the crafts market in Petit Thouars in Miraflores is worth visiting) expect to bargain. Stall holders are ready with their "bottom price." Even in shops if you make an offer, politely, no one will be offended.

Taxis

Taxis in Lima are relatively cheap. They are even cheaper in other cities. If you stop a car in the street, arrange a price before you get in. You should have no trouble getting a taxi driver to stick to this. Be careful getting a taxi late at night. If you prefer, there are telephone taxi services that cost slightly more but offer greater security like Taxi Real. Get telephone numbers from your hotel.

Police

Peru has introduced a 24-hour tourist help-line for complaints or advice. The number is posted at the airport as you arrive in Lima. Usually there is a tourist office in the more popular destinations like Cusco or during important fiestas, like Holy Week in Ayacucho.

ADDRESSES AND CONTACTS

Embassy of Peru,
215 Lexington Avenue, 21st Floor,
New York, NY 10016
Tel: (212) 481-7410

Embassy of Peru,
52 Sloane Street,
London SW1X 9SP
Tel: (0171) 235-1917
(Tourist information available)

South American Explorers Club,
126 Indian Creek Road,
Ithaca, NY 14850
Tel: (607) 277-0488
(also branch in Lima at Avenida Portugal 148 (tel: (511) 425-0142))

Journey Latin America,
14-16 Devonshire Road,
London W4 2BR
Tel: (0181) 747-3108
(Specialist travel agents)

Survival International,
11-15 Emerald Street,
London WC1N 3QL
Tel: (0171) 242-1441
(Information on indigenous issues)

Peru Peace Network,
PO Box 551,
Jefferson City, MO 65102-0551
Tel: (314) 636-8979
perupeace@igc.apc.org

Peru Support Group,
Fenner Brockway House,
37-39 Great Guildford Street,
London SE1 0ES
Tel: (0171) 620-1103

FURTHER READING AND BOOKSTORES

Crabtree, J., *Peru Under García: An Opportunity Lost*, London and Pittsburgh, 1992.
Durand, F., *Business and Politics in Peru: The State and the National Bourgeoisie,* Boulder, CO, 1994.
Flores Galindo, A., *Buscando un Inca: identidad y utopia en los Andes,* Lima, 1987.
Hemming, J., *The Conquest of the Incas,* London, 1983.
Jenkins, D., *Peru: The Rough Guide,* London and New York, 1997.
Mariátegui, J.C., Seven Interpretive Essays on Peruvian Society, Texas, 1971.
Poole, D. and G. Rénique, *Peru: Time of Fear,* London, 1992.
Reid, M., *Peru: Paths to Poverty,* London, 1985.
Scott Palmer, D. (ed), *Shining Path of Peru,* London, 1992.
Stark, O, Degregori, C.I., and R. Kirk (eds), *The Peru Reader,* Durham, NC and London, 1995.
Thorp, R. and G. Bertram, *Peru 1890-1977: Growth and Policy in an Open Economy,* Basingstoke, 1978.
Vargas Llosa, M. et al, *Vargas Llosa for President,* London, 1991.

Fiction and Poetry

Arguedas, J. M., *Todas las sangres,* Lima, 1964.
Bryce Echenique, A., *A World for Julius,* Texas, 1992.
Vallejo, C., *Collected Poems of César Vallejo,* London, 1970.
Vargas Llosa, M., *Aunt Julia and the Scriptwriter,* London and New York, 1982.
Vargas Llosa, M., *Conversation in the Cathedral,* New York, 1975.

To read Peruvian newspapers and weekly magazines like *Caretas,* as well as all the latest government and non-governmental organization web pages, go to the home page of the Red Científica Peruana (http://www.rcp.net.pe/rcp.html).

Local Bookstores

Librería Delta,
N de Piérola 689,
Lima

The Book Exchange,
Ocoña 211,
Lima

Librería Studium,
Plaza Francia 1164,
Lima
(also branch at Mesón de la Estrella 144, Cusco)

Los Andes,
Portal Comercio 125,
Cusco

FACTS AND FIGURES

GEOGRAPHY

Official name: República del Perú.

Surface Area: 496,225 sq. miles (1,285, 216 km²): Peru is the 19th largest country in the world.

Situation: On the central western coast of South America, bordered by Ecuador and Colombia to the north, Brazil and Bolivia to the east, and Chile to the south.

Administrative structure: Divided into 24 departments and one constitutional province.

Capital: Lima, population 7.5 million (1996 estimate).

Other principal cities (population x 1,000 1995 estimates): Arequipa (634), Trujillo (532), Callao (515) Chiclayo (426), Piura (324), Chimbote (296), Cusco (275), Iquitos (269), Huancayo (207).

Infrastructure: 28,350 miles of roads, of which 22 per cent are national highways. Between 1992 and 1996, 1,300 miles of road were repaired and improved, including sections of the main trunk road in the country, the Panamerican Highway, which runs for more than 1,150 miles down the coast. Only 11 per cent of roads are all-weather (1995). There are eight stretches of Peruvian railroads stretching a total 820 miles. Most of these were earmarked for privatization in 1997, including the Central Andean railroad that links Lima's neighboring port of Callao with the mining center, La Oroya, with what is known as the highest railroad in the world. Peru also has 60 airports, of which the main one is Lima's Jorge Chávez International Airport, 12 seaports, and 4 river ports. The ports owned by state company, Enapu, are also scheduled to be privatized.

Relief, landscape and climate: The *costa* or coastal region covers about 10% of Peru's territory, comprised of a narrow ribbon of desert, approximately 870 miles long. Extremely low average rainfall (approx. 1.6 inches) accounts for widespread aridity, although irrigation from some 50 rivers which drain from the Andes allows agriculture in an area of 1.5 million acres. Low mean temperatures are the result of high atmospheric pressure in the southeast Pacific and the cold Humboldt ocean current. A warm surface current, El Niño, sometimes replaces colder water, bringing heavy rains and considerable damage to crops. About 60% of Peruvians live in the *costa*, which includes the seven largest cities in the country. The sierra or highlands accounts for 26% of the country's area, stretching from the Bolivian border in the south to the frontier with Ecuador in the north. The sierra runs parallel to the coast, as close as 60 miles at some points. The high plains of the south and central Peruvian Andes range from 12,000 to 14,000 feet and are too high for agriculture, although llamas and alpacas are reared there. There are ten mountains over 18,000 feet; the highest is Huascarán at 22,204 feet. To the south of the sierra range are Peru's volcanoes. Most agriculture is located in deep river valleys, where potatoes and grains can be cultivated. Temperatures at 9,000 feet can vary widely around the mean annual average of 57°F, and frosts are common. Rainfall is highly unpredictable, leading to droughts and flooding. Approximately 35% of the population lives in the sierra, overwhelmingly of indigenous origin. The selva or jungle covers

Departments of Peru

QUITO ■

ECUADOR

COLOMBIA

Tumbes ●
TUMBES

AMAZONAS

Iquitos ●

LORETO

PIURA

Piura ◉

Moyobamba
Chachapoyas ●

LAMBAYEQUE

CAJAMARCA

SAN
MARTÍN

BRAZIL

Chiclayo ◉

Cajamarca ●

LA LIBERTAD

Trujillo ◉

Pucallpa ●

ANCASH

HUÁNUCO

Huaráz ●

Huánuco ●

PASCO

UCAYALI

Cerro de Pasco ●

LIMA

JUNIN

MADRE DE DIOS

CALLAO ● Callao

LIMA ■

Huancayo ●

Puerto
Maldonado ●

HUANCAVELICA

CUSCO

Huancavelica ●

Ayacucho ●

Abancay ●

Cuzco ●

● Ica

AYACUCHO

APURÍMAC

PUNO

ICA

Lake
Titicaca

AREQUIPA

Puno ◉

Arequipa ◉

MOQUEGUA

LA PAZ ■

Moquegua ●

BOLIVIA

TACNA

Tacna ●

CHILE

PACIFIC OCEAN

N

■	capital city
◉	city
PASCO	departments
—·—·	national boundary
— — —	department boundary
——	river

0   km   250

0   miles   250

64% of the country, but contains only 5% of its population. It includes a wide range of habitats and landscapes, ranging from cloud forest to lowland jungle or rainforest. There are few roads, and rivers provide the main means of transport. Higher rates of rainfall encourage dense vegetation, especially in the Amazon Basin.

Flora and fauna: Peru has one of the world's richest collections of wildlife, containing dozens of unique habitats. In the coastal region, land animals and plants are scarce, but sea life is extraordinarily diverse, including gulls, pelicans, cormorants, and penguins, as well as dolphins and sea lions. The sierra is home to a wide range of animals, the most common being vicuñas, alpacas, and llamas. Rarer species include pumas, wolves, and bears, while chinchillas, squirrels, and rabbit-like viscachas all inhabit particular areas of the sierra. Bird life is also rich, and eagles, hawks, and Andean condors, with nine-feet wingspans, can be seen in the region. The selva is the most naturally diverse region of the country, containing thousands of animal, bird, and plant species. River banks and flood plains contain caymans, toucans, macaws, and horned screamer, while the dense jungle is home to pecaries, tapirs, tree sloths, and the spotted jaguar, the second largest cat in the world.

POPULATION

Population: 22.6 million (1993 census); estimated population in 1996: 24.3 million.

Annual population growth: 1.7% (1996); 2.4% (1980s).

Urbanization: 70.1% live in urban areas, 29.9% in rural areas (1993 census). In 1961, 47.4 % lived in urban areas and 52.6% in rural areas.

Population by age (1996): 35.4% 14 or under; 56.5% under 25 years old.

Infant mortality (1996): 50 per 1,000 live births; in rural areas 83 per 1,000 births; in Huancavelica department in the central sierra, 102 per 1,000.

Maternal mortality (1996): 261 per 100,000 births.

Percentage of births with health professional present (1996): 53%; in urban areas: 74%; in rural areas: 19%.

Poverty (1996): 49% per cent of population was classified as poor and 18% as living in extreme poverty (more than 4 million people, of whom 36% live in urban areas and 64% in rural areas).

Services (1995): only 25% of those living in extreme poverty had access to health services, while 73% had access to education, mainly primary education; overall, 62% of homes had access to potable water and 65% to electricity.

Life expectancy (1995): 67.6 years.

Education: Education is theoretically free and compulsory between the ages of 6 and 15, but drop-out rates are high. Enrol-ment at primary level is estimated at 97%, but at secondary level falls to 65%. There are 46 universities, but access is limited to a small minority.

Illiteracy (1995): 10.5%; (1993 census) men: 7%; women: 18%; men in rural areas: 17%; women in rural areas: 43%.

Percentage of women in Congress (1995): 11% .

Social development index (UNDP Human Develop-ment Index 1996): 91st position out of 174 positions (USA 2nd, UK 16th position).

Languages: Spanish and Quechua (official); Aymara; several dozen other lan-guages spoken by inhabit-ants of Amazon basin.

Religion: Roman Catholic: 89%; Evangelical: 3%; other Christian: 2%.

HISTORY AND POLITICS

Key historical dates:
20,000-10,000 BC: first evidence of human settlement in Peru * 1000-200 BC: period of Chavín culture * 200-1100 AD: classical pre-Columbian cultures emerge * 1438-1532: expansion of Inca empire from Cusco * 1532: Francisco Pizarro lands at Tumbes * 1533 : execution of Atahualpa * 1535: Lima founded * 1572: Spanish invade last Inca enclave at Vilcabamba, Túpac Amaru executed * 1780: uprising against Spanish led by Túpac Amaru II * 1821: Peru declares independence * 1824: final defeat of Royalists * 1854: abolition of slavery * 1879-83: war of the Pacific with Chile *1919-30: dictatorship of Augusto Leguía *1928: Mariátegui founds Peruvian Communist Party * 1930: Haya de la Torre founds APRA * 1932: APRA insurrection at Trujillo * 1968-1975: radical military regime of Gen. Juan Velasco * 1970: catastrophic avalanche kills 70,000 at Yungay * 1980: second term of Fernando Belaúnde; beginning of Shining Path insurgency * 1984: MRTA begins armed campaign * 1985: election of Alán García * 1990: electoral victory of Alberto Fujimori * 1992: capture of Shining Path leader, Abimael Guzmán * 1995: Fujimori wins second term * December 1996: Lima hostage crisis begins * April 1997: military attack ends embassy siege.

Constitution: Presidential republic. President is elected by popular vote every five years. Unicameral Congress of 120 seats elected by popular vote also every five years.

Head of state: President Alberto Fujimori.

Main political formations (with number of seats in Congress since April 1995): Cambio 90 (67); Unión por el Perú (17); APRA (8); Frente Independiente Moralista (6); others (22).

Armed forces (1996): army 75,000 (including 50,000 conscripts); navy 18,000 (13,500 conscripts); air force 15,000 (2,000 conscripts); paramilitary personnel 70,000. Military spending (1994): 1.8% of GDP.

Membership of international organizations (1997): UN and UN organizations; Organization of American States; Latin America Integration Association.

Media and communications: 45 daily newspapers, many provincial. *El Comercio* and *Expreso* are conservative, while *La República* is more left-wing. There is one main state-owned television channel and 6 private channels. Around 4 million homes have a television. Peru has approximately 300 radio stations.

Telephone density (1996): 5.2 phone lines per 100 inhabitants.

ECONOMY

GDP (1996): $50 billion .
GDP per capita (1996): $2,025 (1996).
Currency unit: sol. 2.60 soles = US$1 (1996).
Real GDP growth: 1992: -4.5%; 1993: 6.4%; 1994: 12.8%; 1995: 6.9%; 1996: 2.8%.

Real GDP by economic activity (1994): manufacturing: 23.4%; commerce 13.4%; agriculture 12.8%; mining 8.9%; construction 8%; fishing 1.6%; electrical power 1.6%; others 30.3%.

Inflation: 1992: 56.7%; 1993: 39.5%; 1994: 15.3%; 1995: 10.2%; 1996: 11.8%.
Foreign debt (1996): $33.5 billion.
Exports (1996): $5.9 billion.
Imports (1996): $7.8 billion.
Trade balance (1996): -$1.9

billion.
Income from privatization (May 1992-April 1997): $7.1 billion.
Total registered direct foreign investment (1996): $5.5 billion.
Principal countries with registered direct investments (1996): Spain: $2.2 billion; UK: $1 billion; USA: $797 million; Netherlands: $304 million; Chile: $222 million.
Main exports (1996): minerals (copper, gold, etc.) $2.65 billion; fishmeal $909 million; textiles $454 million; coffee $223 million.
Selected imports (1996): vehicles $237 million; wheat $243 million; crude oil $426 million; sugar $116 million.
Main trading partners (1996):
Principal destinations of Peruvian exports: USA 19.8%; UK 7.3%; China 7.2%; Japan 6.6%; Germany 5.1%.
Principal origins of Peruvian imports: USA 26%; Colombia 8.7%; Venezuela 7.6%; Japan 5.2%; Brazil: 4.6%.

PERU AND THE UNITED STATES/BRITAIN

In 1996 the U.S. government allotted $91 million in aid to Peru, including $15.5 million for anti-narcotics programs. The provisional figure of $112.7 million for 1997 includes an increase to $25 million for anti-drug programs. The "war on drugs" continues to be the main issue within U.S. policy towards Peru, and the Fujimori government is keen to appear cooperative, winning full "certification" and hence access to aid in 1996 and 1997. The USA is Peru's main trading partner, accounting for almost 20% of exports and 26% of imports in 1996, although its importance has declined over several decades.

The UK government gives small amounts of bilateral aid to Peru, largely in health and education projects.

Britain is one of Peru's main export markets, and in 1995 Peru achieved a trade surplus with the UK of $313 million. British companies have invested in Peru's privatization program, and according to *El Comercio,* the UK is currently the second largest direct investor in the Peruvian economy, buying shares in the energy, mining, and telecommunications sectors.